Research and Compiled By
Matthew Balent

Editor
Alex Marciniszyn

Illustrators
Ed Kwiatkowski
Michael Kucharski
Kevin Siembieda

Art Direction
Kevin Siembieda

Keylining
Matthew Balent

Typist
Maryann Siembieda

Publisher
Palladium Books

TABLE OF CONTENTS

Page	
4	Weapons
4	Bo Staff
5	Parrying Weapons
5	Chain Weapons
6	Japanese Battle Axe
6-7	Sickle Weapons
7-9	Swords and Knives
10	Japanese Grapple
10-11	Spears
12	Japanese Arrow-heads
12	Iron Smoking Pipes
12	Iron War Fans
13-27	Japanese Armour
28-30	Chinese Armour
30	Korean Armour
31	Malaysian Armour
32-41	Japanese Fortifications
42-47	Chinese Fortifications
48	Map of Eastern Asia
49	Bibliography

This work is dedicated to my friends Jean and Helene on the occasion of their graduation.

FORWARD

This book is designed to be an introduction to the various weapons, armour, and defensive works found in oriental culture, although written with the fantasy gamer in mind. Anyone who is interested in these topics should find the book useful. Gamers who are interested in incorporating an oriental based culture in their campaigns will find ample material to get them going. The ideas presented in this book are somewhat of an outgrowth of those contained in **The Palladium Book of Weapons & Armour.** Although ownership of that book is not required further information is provided there for those interested.

WEAPONS

The following is a short description of a few of the weapons used by various oriental cultures. This is by no means a comprehensive list. Further examples can be found in **The Palladium Book of Weapons & Armour** Each of the weapons is given a set of numerical values which are explained below.

Name - Self Explanatory.
Type - The general group to which the weapon belongs. The groups are hafted (H), Knives (K), Miscellaneous (M), Pole Arms (P), Spears (Sp), and Swords (Sw).
Swords - The length of the weapon in meters.
Mass - The mass of the weapon in kilograms.
Dex. - A relative indication of how "quick" a weapon is based on balance, mass, etc. The lower this number the better.
Parry - A relative indication of how easily the weapon can parry other attacks. The higher the number the better.
Attack Types - Not all weapons were designed for the same purpose. The four basic attack types are cut, chop, thrust, and impact. The main differences between a cut and a chop are the sharpness and curvature of the blade.
Symmetry - Being that any weapon can be thrown, this is a relative indication of how effective the arm would be as a missile, the lower the number the better.
Damage - A relative indication of how much damage this weapon would cause to an "average" target.
Other - Notes of interest about the weapon, usually the geographical area of origin. A (T) in this column indicated the weapon is primarily used with two hands.

On all illusrations of edged weapons, ("''''') indicates which portion of the blade is sharp.

Name	Type	Length	Mass	Dex	Parry	Attack Types	Sym.	Damage
Bo	M	2.8m	1.4kg	1	2	Impact	2	2
Japanese Staff (T)								

The use of wooden staves or clubs in combat is ancient indeed, for they represent a transition from unarmed to armed conflicts. The Japanese employed a number of staves of various sizes and construction; many were made almost entirely of iron or steel. Being relatively harmless, for training purposes, the techniques of staff combat were taught in almost every sword and spear school as a prelude to the use of the more deadly weapons. In many instances it is impossible to distinguish between staff and sword techniques.

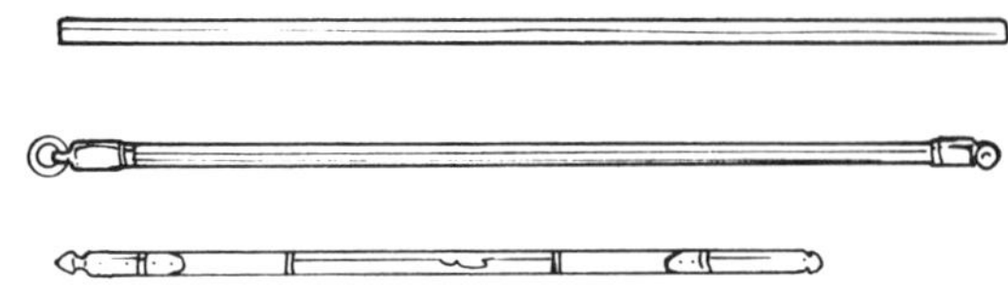

Name	Type	Length	Mass	Dex.	Parry	Attack Types	Sym.	Damage
Jitte	M	.5m	1.4kg	0	3	Thrust/impact	2	2
Japanese Parrying Weapon								
Tjabang	M	.5m	1.1kg	0	3	Thrust/Impact	2	2
Malaysian Parrying Weapon								

The origin of these weapons is a matter of debate but they are certainly designed to deprive an opponent of his sword. The techniques used ranged from parries against sword strikes to blows directed against the opponent's eyes, throat and abdomen. Mastery of these weapons depended heavily on being able to evade the enemy's sword, which in turn lead to parries, which in turn lead to counterstrikes.

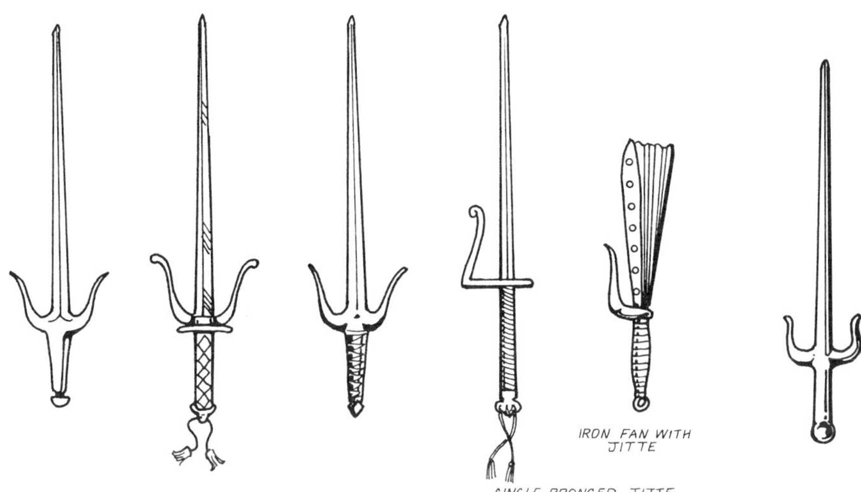

EXAMPLES OF JITTES

TJABANG
COMMON TO MALASIA AND THE PHILIPPINES.

Name	Type	Length	Mass	Dex.	Parry	Attack Types	Sym.	Damage
Kau Sin Ke	M	1.1m	.6kg	2	2	Impact	3	1
Chinese Whipping Chain (T)								
Kusarigama	M	2.2m	1.5kg	2	3	Chop	2	2
Japanese Chain Weapon (T)								

Chain weapons, of which the Kusarigama is but one, were noted for their effectiveness in neutralizing an opponent's sword or spear. These weapons could also be used to entangle an opponent's legs to help unbalance him. Once the enemy had been neutralized by the chain, the weapon attached to it could be used to finish the job. Obviously, these weapons required a certain amount of space around the wielder and would be nearly useless in a confined area.

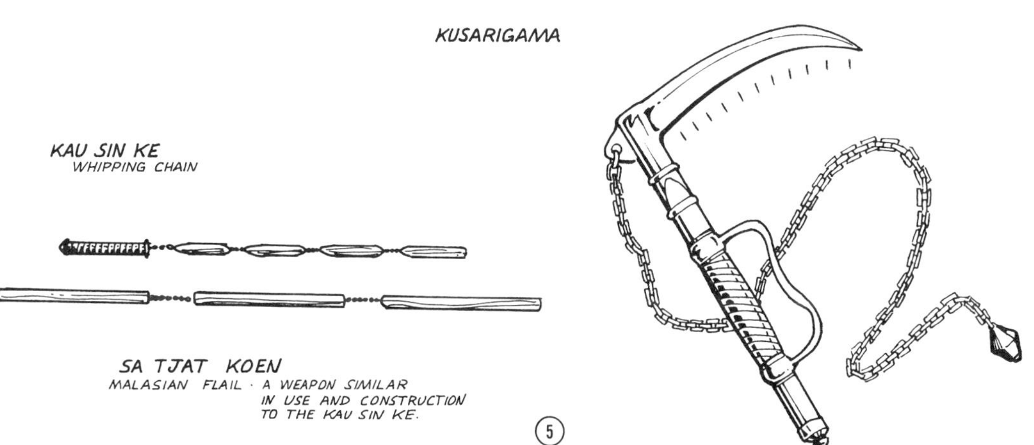

KUSARIGAMA

KAU SIN KE
WHIPPING CHAIN

SA TJAT KOEN
MALASIAN FLAIL · A WEAPON SIMILAR IN USE AND CONSTRUCTION TO THE KAU SIN KE.

Name	Type	Length	Mass	Dex.	Parry	Attack Types	Sym.	Damage
Masakari	H	.8m	1.9kg	1	2	Chop	2	3

Japanese Battle Axe

The Japanese tended to use weapons which were designed to cut and thrust. Battle axes and other heavy smashing weapons were generally not used. As with many other weapons a chain was often attached to the handle in an effort to give the wielder an advantage over sword or spear armed foes.

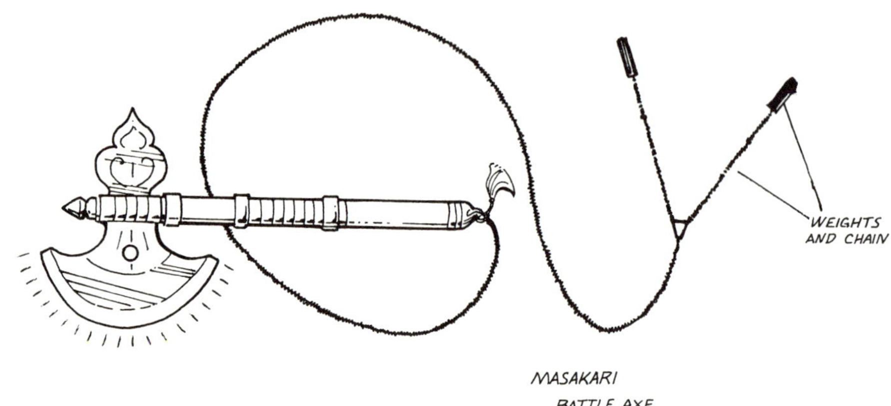

MASAKARI
BATTLE AXE

Name	Type	Length	Mass	Dex.	Parry	Attack Types	Sym.	Damage
Kama	H	.5m	1.0kg	0	2	Chop	2	2

Japanese Rice Sickle

Because of the rather strick rules which existed during the Feudal Period in Japan concerning swords, spears, and other obvious weapons many combat arts were invented which centered around the use of rather simple tools. The Kama was one such tool which was used as a weapon.

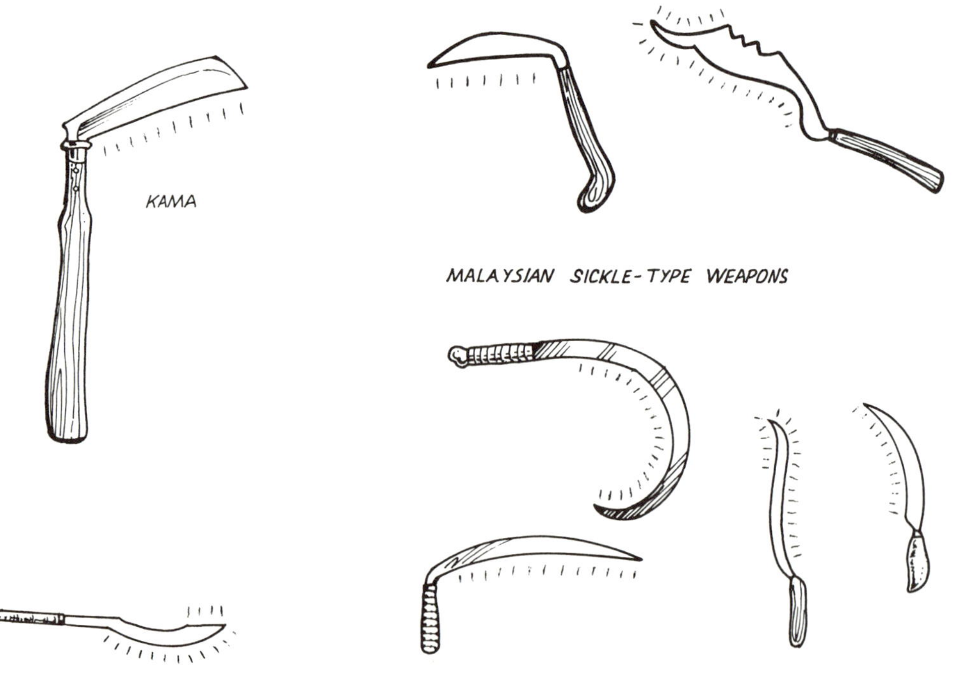

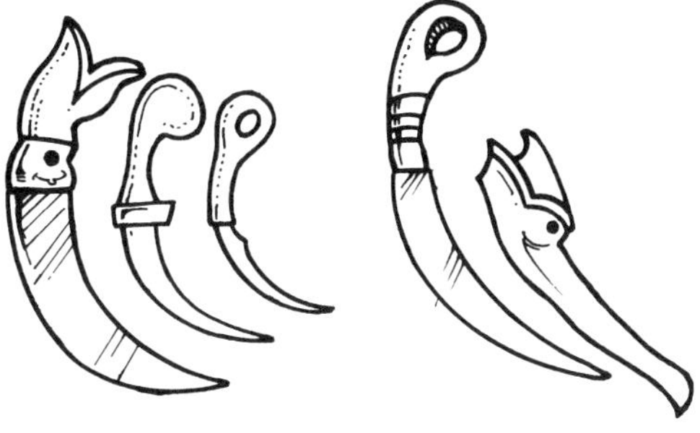

MALAYSIAN "TIGER CLAW" WEAPONS

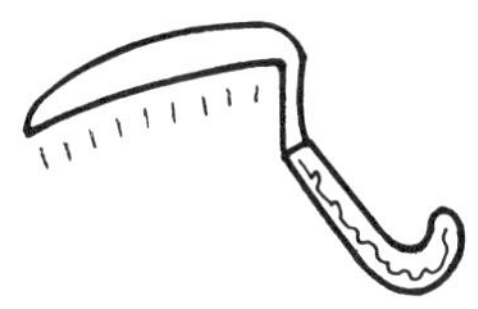

SABIT - TYPE
AGRICULTURAL TOOLS/WEAPONS

Name	Type	Length	Mass	Dex.	Parry	Attack Types	Sym.	Damage
Pedang	Sw	.6m	.8kg	0	3	Cut/Chop/Thrust	3	2
Malaysia								
Arit	M	.4m	.3kg	1	1	Chop	2	1

The fighting arts of the **Malaysian** and **Phillipine** areas were often as well advanced as those employed in Japan and China. They employed swords and staves, knives and spears, as well as more exotic arms such as whipping chains in addition to their basic unarmed combat styles. As there was a certain amount of intermingling of all of the oriental cultures, weapons and martial arts from different areas often were found being used in countries other than their original.

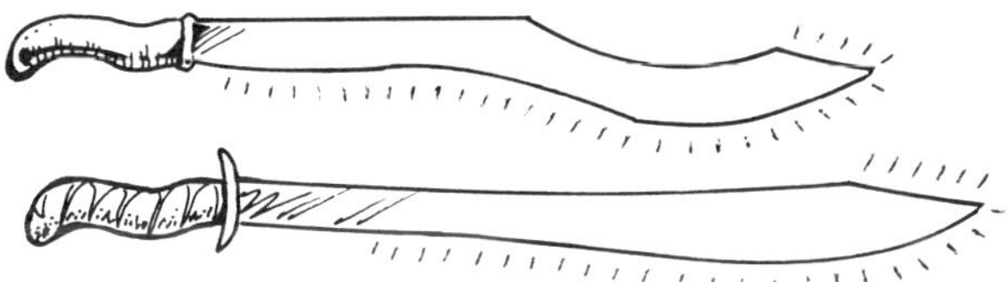

TWO TYPICAL STYLES OF THE PEDANG SWORD

ARIT

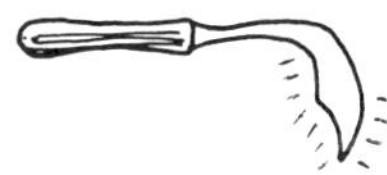

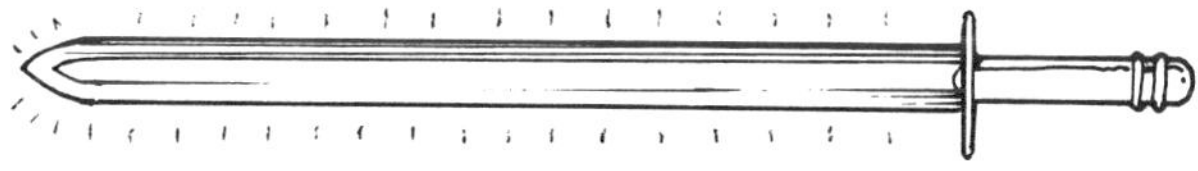

IN COMPARISON IS A CHINESE SWORD

OTHER MALAYSIAN
SWORDS

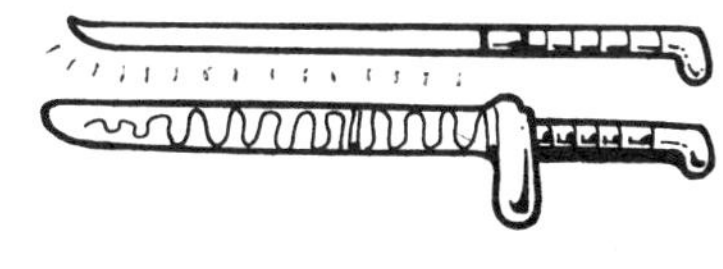

SAKIN AND SHEATH

PARANG -TYPE SWORD

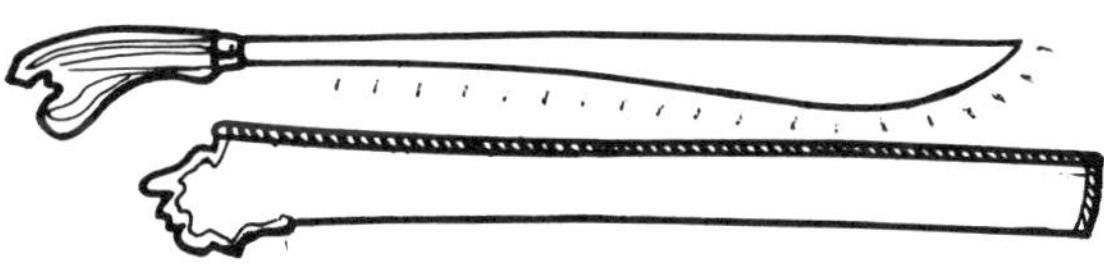

SIKIM GALA AND SHEATH

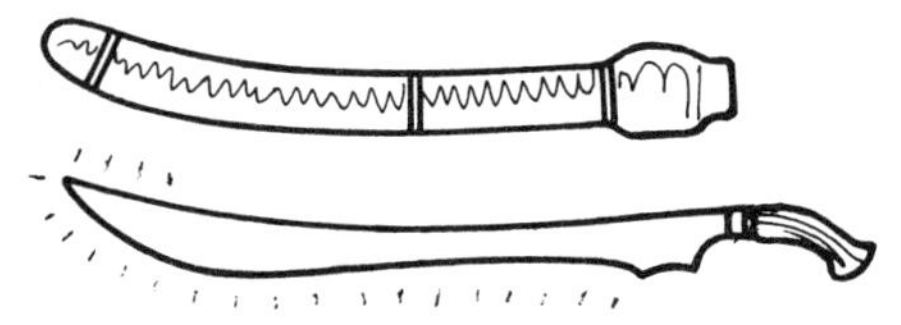

GADUBONG AND SHEATH

TAPAK KUDAK

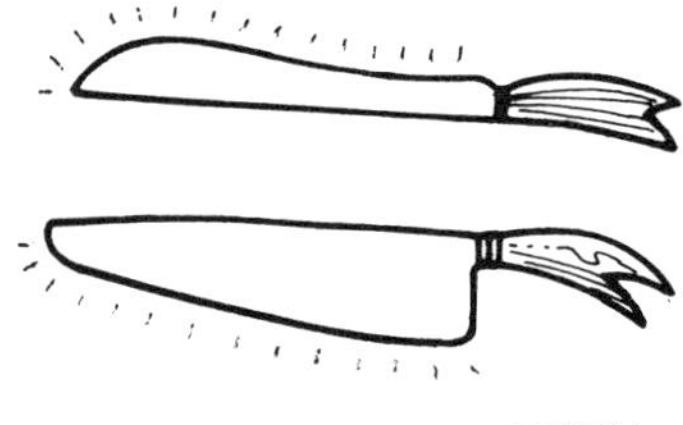

THININ

MALAYSIAN KNIVES

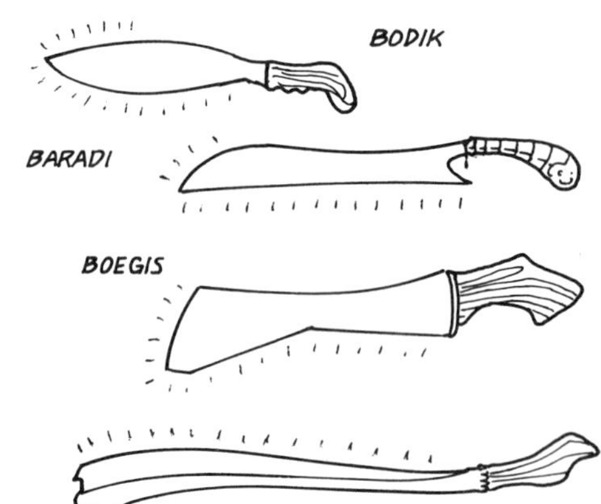

BODIK

BARADI

BOEGIS

KELEWANG

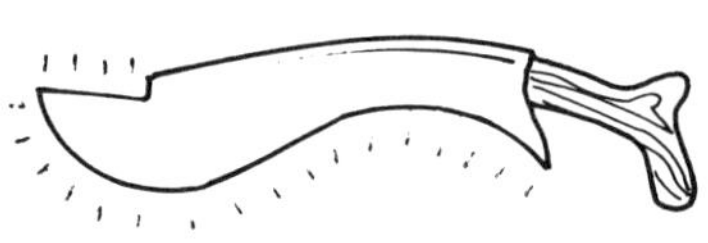

LARBANGO

MENTĀWĀ

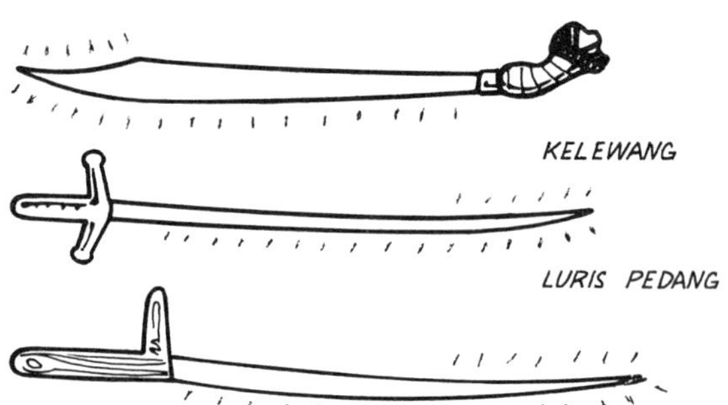

KELEWANG

LURIS PEDANG

PEUDEUENG

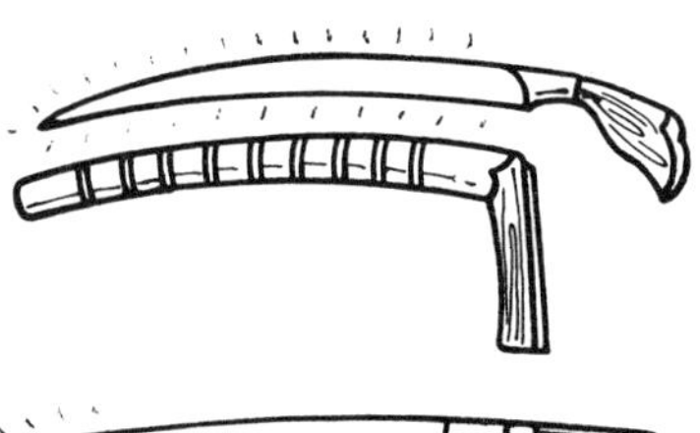

TWO SEWAR AND SHEATHS

JAPANESE SWORD DRAWING EXERCISE / TECHNIQUE

Name	Type	Length	Mass	Dex	Parry	Attack Types	Sym.	Damage
Katana Japanese	Sw	1.1m	1.4kg	1	3	Cut/Thrust	2	3
Wakizashi Japanese	Sw	.6m	.8kg	0	2	Cut/Thrust	2	2

These two weapons made up a warrior's **Daisho**, or "The long and the short." As with other Japanese weapons there were a number of variations of these swords. The quality of the workmanship of these weapons is legendary and most often a warrior's swords were family heirlooms handed down from generations past.

There was a rather formal etiquette centered around the sword. The manner in which they were worn, handled, the color of the scabbard, and numerous other things all had specific meaning. As with the other weapons there were innumerable styles of **kenjutsu**, the art of the sword. Variations often employed both swords at once (**nito-kentutsu**). An outgrowth of basic sword fighting was **iaijutsu** which was an art based on the initial drawing of the sword so that an often fatal blow could be delivered in one motion in conjunction with the draw. This art was particularly suited to an everyday armed encounter, as opposed to one on the battle field in which weapons were already drawn.

Like the Japanese, the Chinese also developed a variety of sword fighting styles. Usually the training which went into learning to use these weapons was based upon ideas learned from unarmed fighting styles.

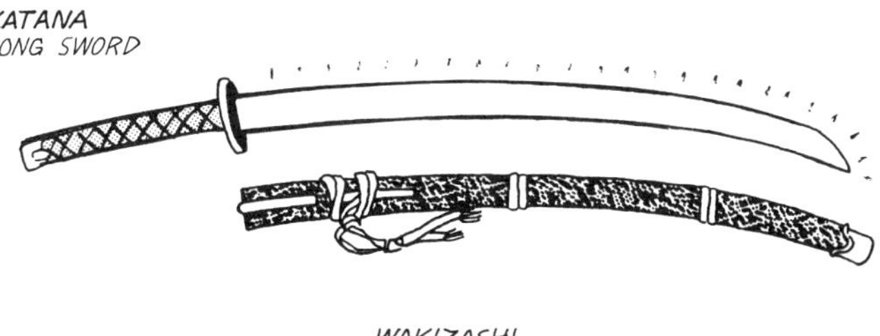

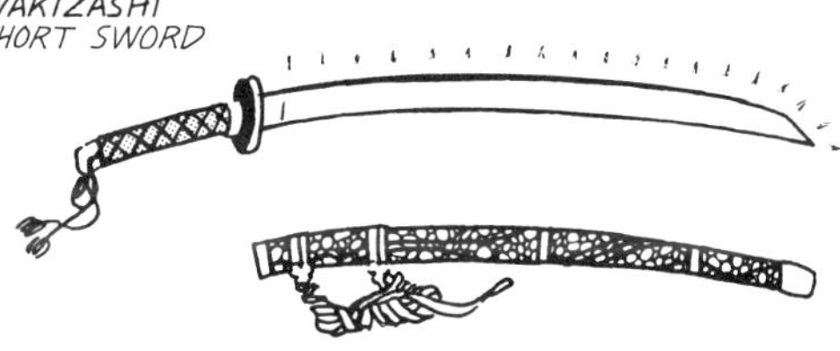

THE PAIR OF SWORDS ARE CALLED DAISHO

THESE ARE ALL SINGLE EDGED BLADES

AIKUCCHI DAGGER WITHOUT HILT

TANTO DAGGER WITH HILT

Name	Type	Length	Mass	Dex	Parry	Attack Types	Sym.	Damage
Kawanga	M	5.0m	3.0kg	2	2	Impact	2	1
Japanese Grapple (T)								

On the battlefield, the Japanese warrior usually carried a rather wide variety of equipment. One of these was the **Kawanaga,** which was attached to his belt. It could be used to tether a horse, secure a boat, secure prisoners, climb walls, or even as a weapon. The multi pointed grapnel on the end of the rope could be used to pull a foe off a horse or to pull at his legs when on foot to make him stumble.

KAWANGA IN COMBAT

Name	Type	Length	Mass	Dex.	Parry	Attack Types	Sym.	Damage
Yari	Sp	2.1m	1.9kg	0	2	Thrust	1	2
Japanese Spear (T)								
Naginata	M	2.2m	2.2kg	1	2	Cut/Thrust	2	3
Japanese Bladed Staff (T)								

The Japanese employed a number of spears and staff weapons in their battles. Like all other Japanese blades, the business ends of these weapons were of the highest quality. The same care in forging which was given to sword blades also went into spear points. The shaft was generally reinforced at points which were put under pressure or were used in parries.

There were two major methods of using these weapons: **Yarijutsu,** the art of the straight spear, and **Naginatajutsu,** the art of the curved spear. Each method was employed using innumerable styles, and specialized styles centered around the specific variation of the weapon the fighter was using.

YARI IN COMBAT

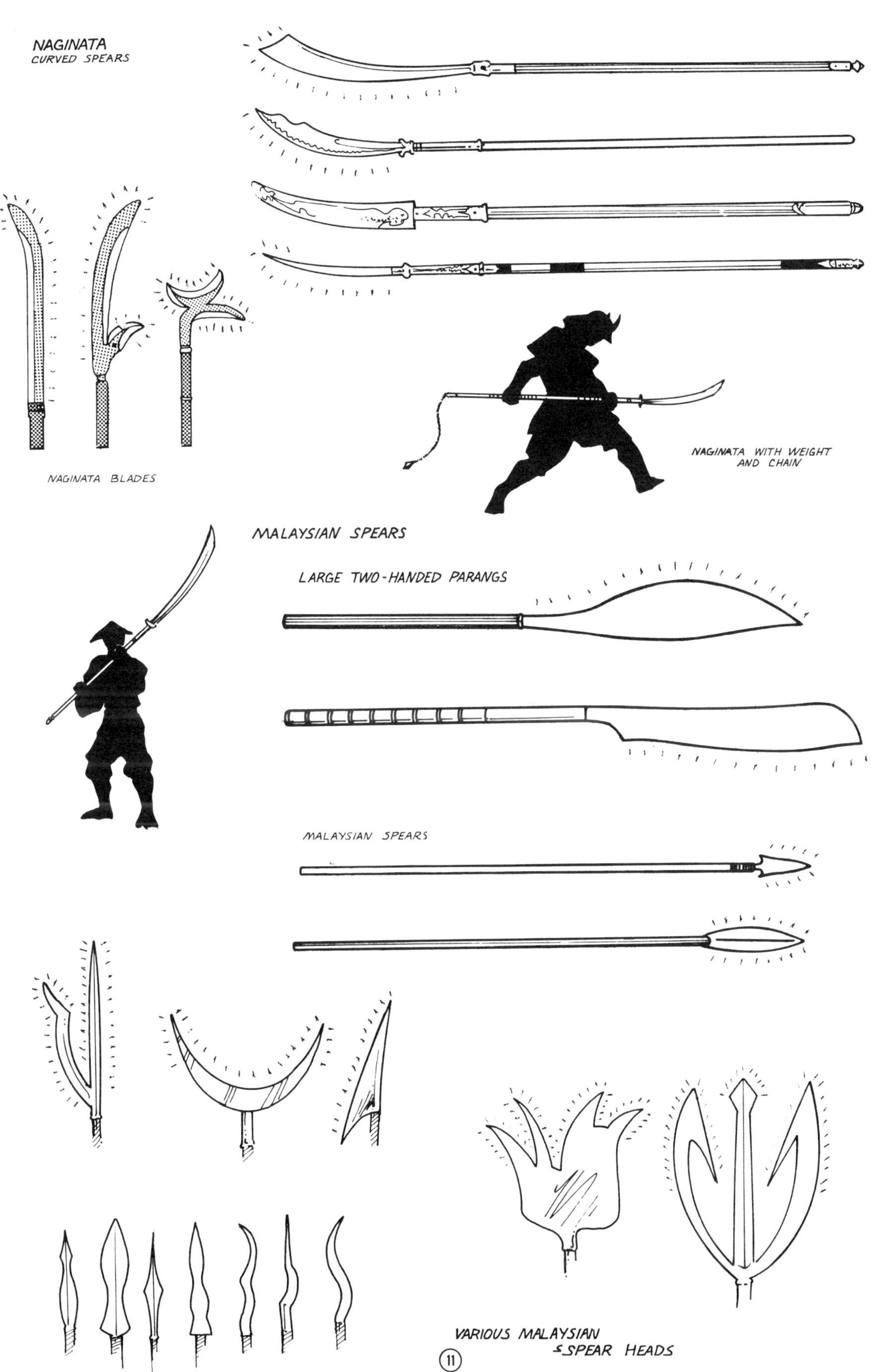
NAGINATA
CURVED SPEARS
NAGINATA BLADES
NAGINATA WITH WEIGHT AND CHAIN
MALAYSIAN SPEARS
LARGE TWO-HANDED PARANGS
MALAYSIAN SPEARS
VARIOUS MALAYSIAN SPEAR HEADS

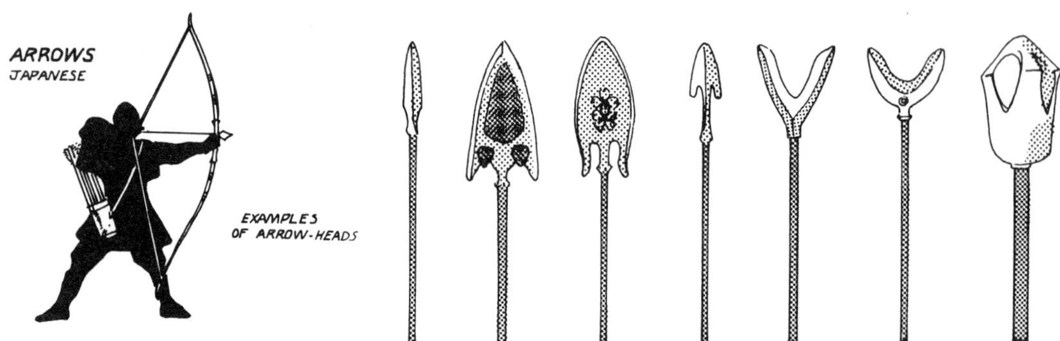

YARI WITH WEIGHTS AND CHAINS ATTACHED

NUMEROUS CHAIN WEAPONS AND WEAPON ATTACHMENTS WERE USED BY THE JAPANESE.

- SEE KUSARIGAMA - AND KAU SIN KE -

Name	Type	Length	Mass	Dex.	Parry	Attack types	Sym.	Damage
Kiseru	M	.8m	1.5kg	0	2	Impact	2	2

Iron Japanese Smoking Pipe

This weapon is another example of a rather simple implement which when in the hands of a trained person could be devastating. This weapon could parry sword strikes as well as deliver effective counterattacks against a foe's head, neck, or abdomen due to its iron construction.

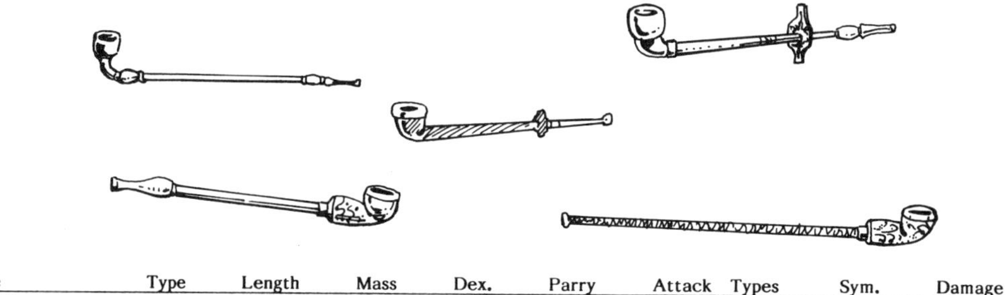

Name	Type	Length	Mass	Dex.	Parry	Attack Types	Sym.	Damage
Gunsen	M	.3m	.5kg	0	2	Impact	1	1

Japanese War Fans

The Japanese used a number of "war fans" which could be either of the folding or non-folding type. These fans were originally used on the battle field to signal troops and to keep cool. When they began to be used as weapons and were constructed of metal, they became very popular. Because weapons were forbidden when one was called to the residence of one's master or a high noble, these items were often life-savers if the noble planned on your death, an occurrence which was not too uncommon.

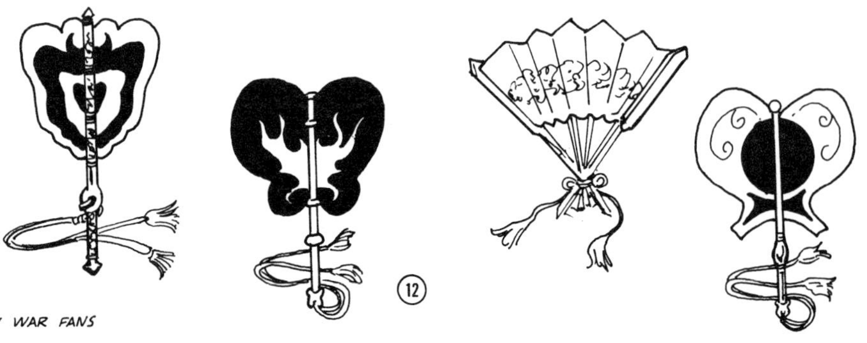

IRON WAR FANS

JAPANESE ARMOUR

Unlike in Europe, the basic form of Japanese armour remained essentially the same over the course of the years. The basic model used by the Japanese consisted of a number of pieces which protected the head, neck, shoulders, arms, chest, abdomen, and the legs. The complete unit tended to be worn by those individuals of high rank, while the poorer warriors settled for partial protection.

The basic model of Japanese armour placed emphasis on lightness and mobility. The heavy types of armour developed by the Europeans were considered a step backward in that they slowed down their wearer. The Japanese realized that a direct hit by an arrow or musket ball would penetrate any reasonable armour worn. The joints and spaces between plates were the normal points of attack in any fight and seeing that these were present in heavy as well as light armour, it is only logical that the Japanese opted to wear armour which did not impede a warrior's ability to evade strikes.

PARTS OF JAPANESE ARMOUR

When reading about Japanese armour it is all too easy to become lost in the maze of technical terms which were used. There are literally hundreds of variations in armour which the Japanese had names for. Every method of lacing, every pattern of mail, all had different names. The following is a short description of the major parts of a suit of Japanese armour listed as they might be put on when preparing for a battle.

The warrior first began with a loincloth (**fundoshi**). A shirt (**shitagi**) resembling an ordinary kimono was put on next and secured with a belt (**obi**). A pair of trousers (**kobakama**)was put on next. A pair of socks (**tabi**), made of leather or cotton, with a division for the big toe were put on next. Over the socks were worn leggins (**kyahan**) of cotton or linen. Sandals (**waraji**) were put on over the tabi and especially in the case of lower ranking warriors, were made of cotton fiber, or palm fiber. Officers often had sandals made of iron or hard leather plates linked together by mail.

The lower legs were protected by a pair of thin guards called **sune-ate.** These were generally made of metal or hard leather sewn onto a padded foundation. Some were of metal only, and were connected together by mail. Either a plate covering the kneecap was attached to the sume-ate or the central vertical strips were extended over this part of the leg.

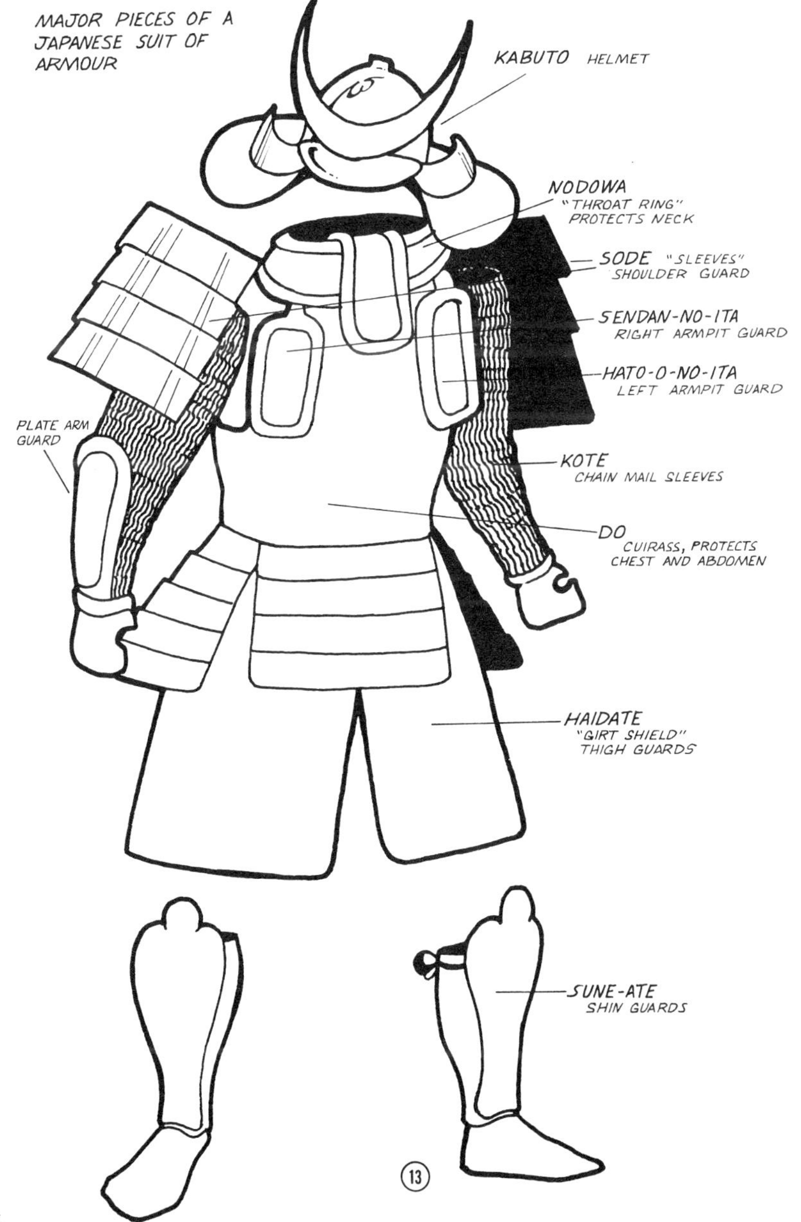

A garment resembling an apron was put on next. Called a **haidate**, this protected the front of the upper legs and was slit up the middle. The haidate could be made of heavy cloth, leather, or metal; the lower edges were generally reinforced with metal or whale bone. It was tied around the waist by cords which were secured in the front.

Next a pair of leather gloves (**yugaky**) were put on. Over these gloves were worn a garment called a **kote.** In general the kote consisted of a close fitting sleeve of padding to which were attached a number of armour plates. This sleeve covered the shoulder, arm and back of the hand. The metal plates were attached together by mail. The inside of the arm was naturally less protected than the outside, and it fell to the skill of the warrior to protect this weak spot from spear thrusts or sword cuts.

The armpits were protected by the **wakibiki** which was contructed of padded mail reinforced by metal splints.

Now the central element of the suit of armour was put on. The **do** or chest protecter was the most important piece in the whole suit. There is an endless variety of these chest protectors which were used at various times in Japan. They were generally made of plates laced or riveted together to cover the four sides of the body from the neck to the upper thighs. The entire garment hung on the body from padded shoulder straps called **kata-ate.** The two major types of do were those which opened in the back **haramaki-do** and those which opened at the side **do-maru**. The better suits of armour had a number of specialized plates which protected the armpits as well as the opening in the back if any.

The warrior then put on an outer belt, **uma-obi** which also served to secure his swords.

The characteristic shoulder guards were put on next. Called **sode,** these pieces were generally made of small scales bound tightly together with silk cords. Underneath the scales was a foundation of leather. The general shape was either retangular or square.

Next the warrior would secure his **daisho** or "the long and the short". The daisho consisted of a long sword, **katana** or **tachi,** and a short sword **wakizashi.** In early times a large sword, called **nodachi** might also have been worn. This was usually strapped to the back.

To protect his neck the warrior would then put on a **gorget** or **nodowa.** These were generally made of scales or plates laced together over a U shaped plate.

The head of a warrior was protected by an elaborate helmet which consisted of a number of different elements. The central dome, **hachi,** followed the general contour of the head. Upon the helmet there was usually a crest or some other identifying symbol. Attached to the basic helmet was a rather large series of plates designed to protect the neck and side of the head. Called the **shikoro,** this piece consisted of a number of metal or leather plates laced together, which hung down from the **hachi.** As with the other parts of the Japanese armour, there are hundreds of different designs and variations of the basic helmet.

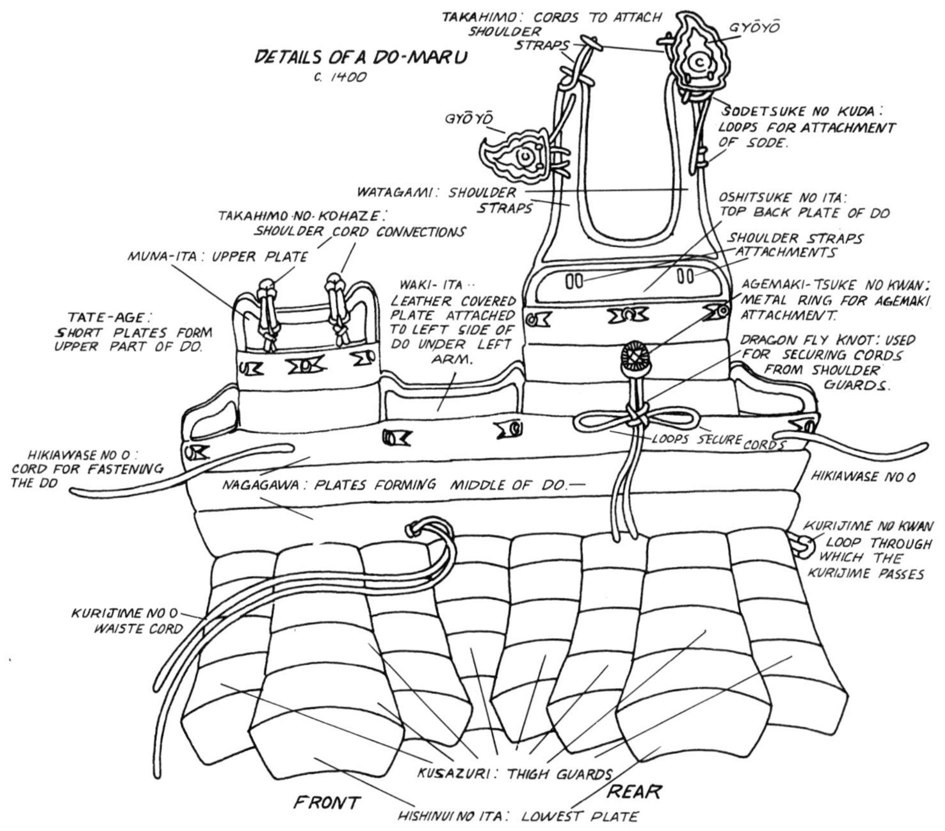

Finally, to protect his face high ranking warriors usually wore a mask of iron, steel, or lacquered leather. These masks (**mempo**) could protect from forehead to chin or only a particular portion of the face. They were generally fastened to a small neck guard which hung over the nodowa. The masks were generally patterned to represent men, demons, or animals. They were generally padded on the inside to give a measure of comfort to the wearer.

MEMPO ARE MADE OF IRON, STEEL, OR LACQUERED LEATHER.

EXAMPLES OF MEMPO
PROTECTIVE FACE MASKS

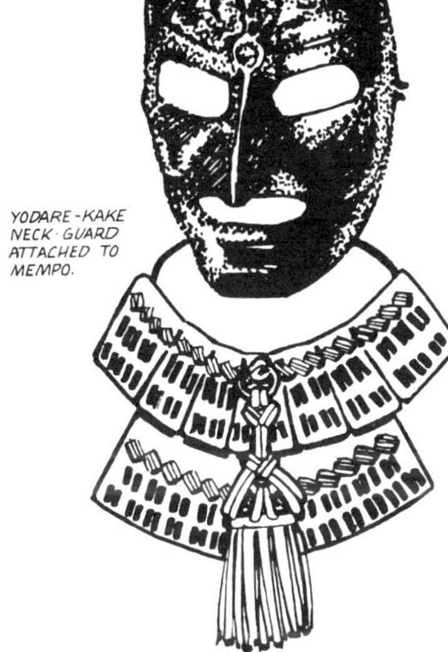

YODARE-KAKE NECK GUARD ATTACHED TO MEMPO.

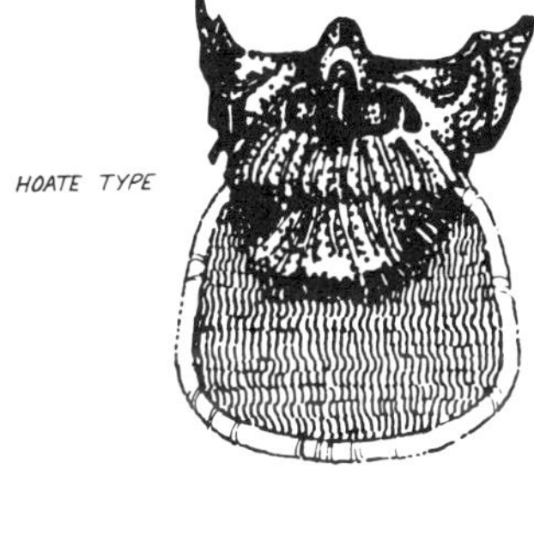

HOATE TYPE

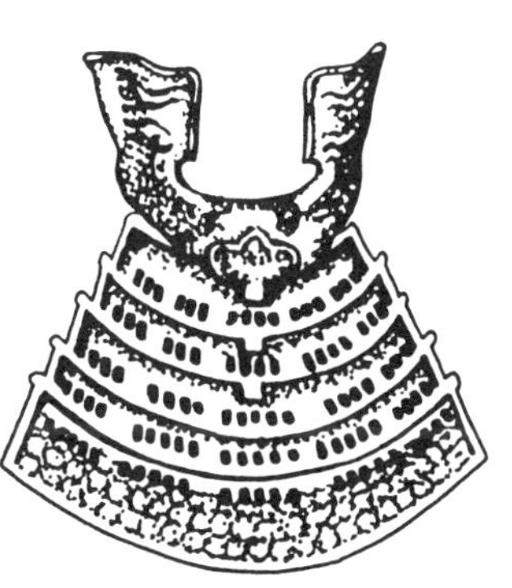

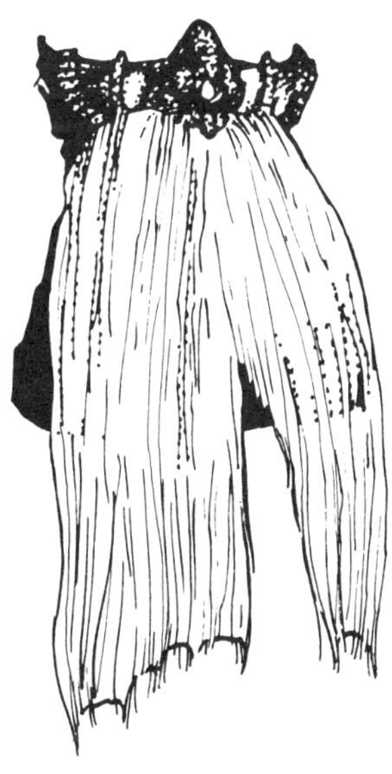

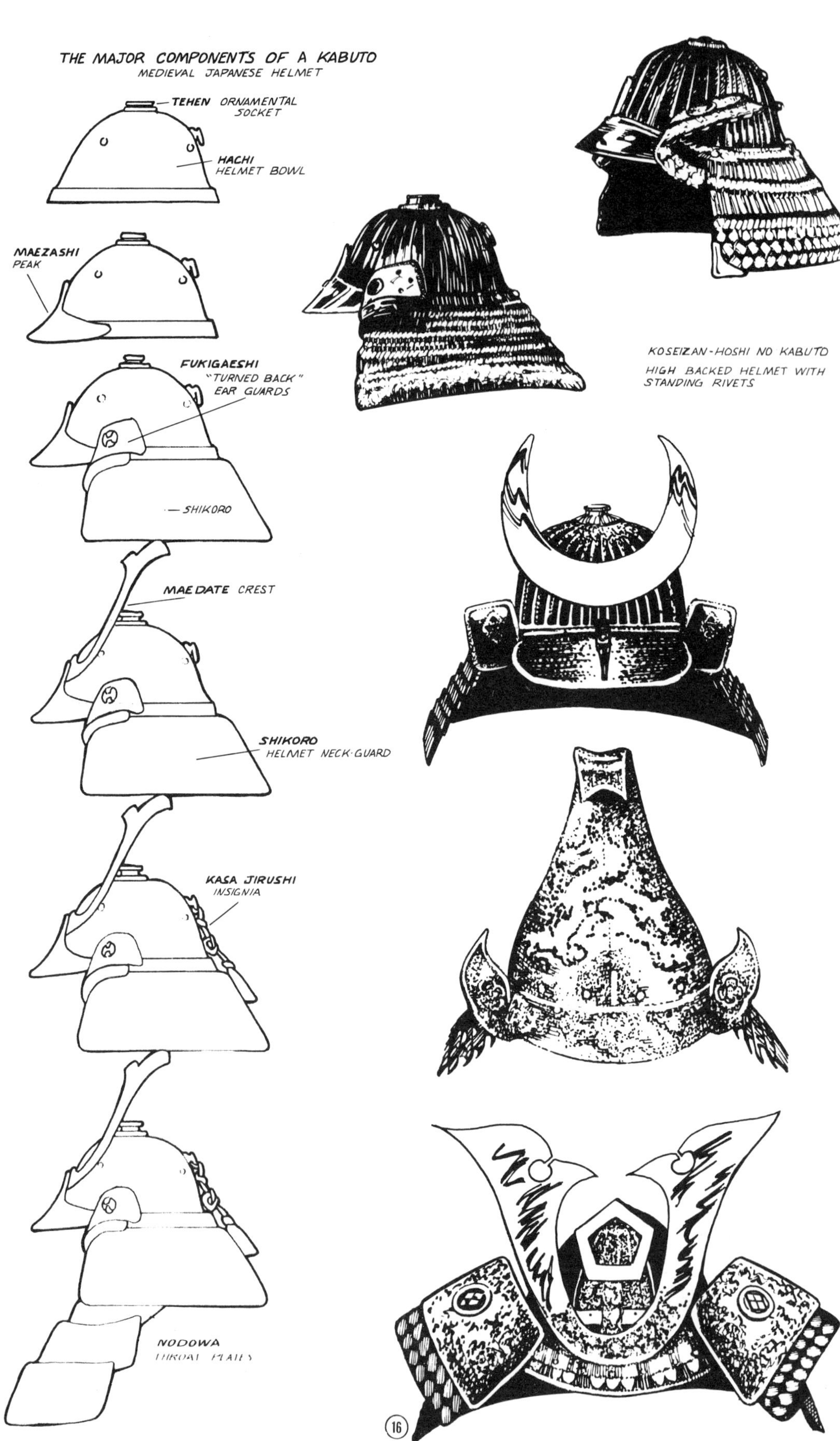

THE MAJOR COMPONENTS OF A KABUTO
MEDIEVAL JAPANESE HELMET
TEHEN ORNAMENTAL SOCKET
HACHI HELMET BOWL
MAEZASHI PEAK
FUKIGAESHI "TURNED BACK" EAR GUARDS
SHIKORO
MAEDATE CREST
SHIKORO HELMET NECK-GUARD
KASA JIRUSHI INSIGNIA
NODOWA THROAT PLATES
KOSEIZAN-HOSHI NO KABUTO
HIGH BACKED HELMET WITH STANDING RIVETS

OTHER FORMS OF ARMOUR

Lower warriors usually could not afford an elaborate suit of armour as described earlier. They were usually content to outfit themselves with as much armour as they could afford, in an effort to prevent themselves from being slaughtered by the more heavily armoured warriors.

One piece of armour usually worn by the lower ranked warriors was the **jingasa.** This was a flat, conical helmet made of steel, iron, or copper. It was generally tied under the chin.

Because of the modular nature of Japanese armour, it was rather easy to wear only part of the complete suit. Often warriors went into battle with only the chest protector. Of course if one was victorious in battle, there were ample opportunities to loot armour from the dead to increase one's own protection.

In addition to the rather heavy armour described earlier, there were also suits of light mail which were worn under normal clothes. This would enable a warrior to go about with some degree of protection without arousing suspicion. The Ninja and warrior monks favored this light armour.

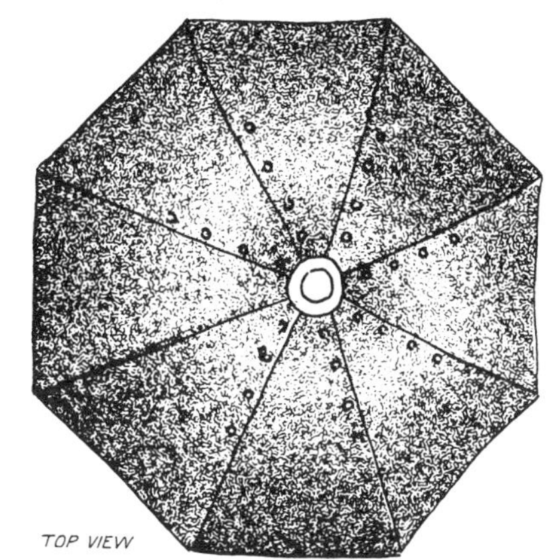

EXAMPLES OF JINGASA HELMETS

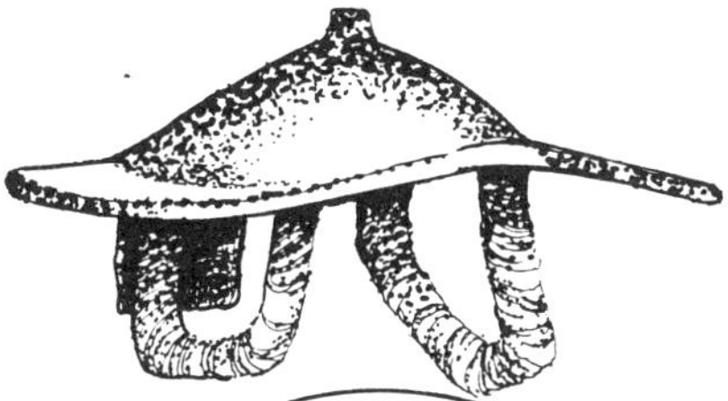

TOP VIEW

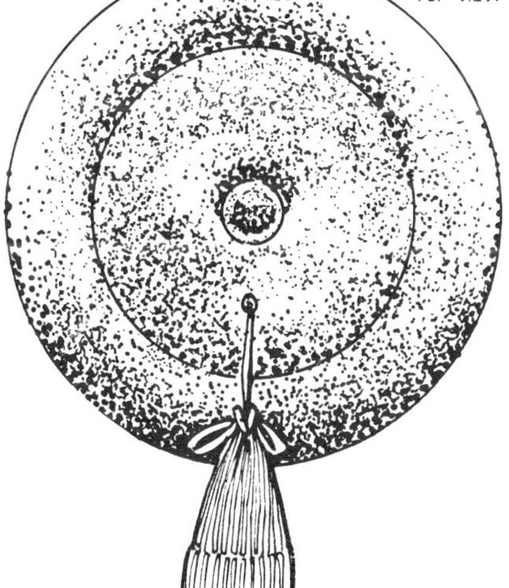

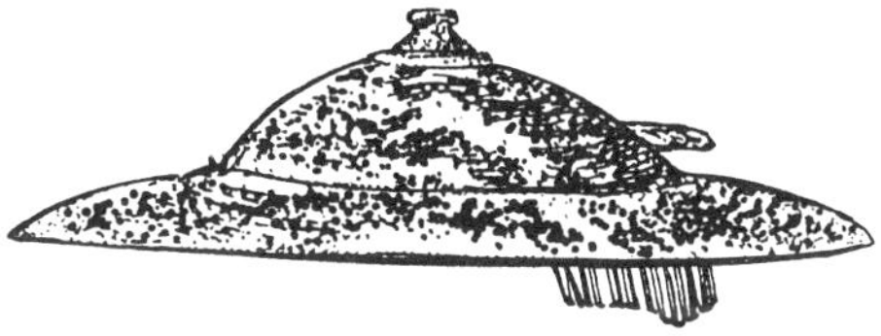

TOP VIEW

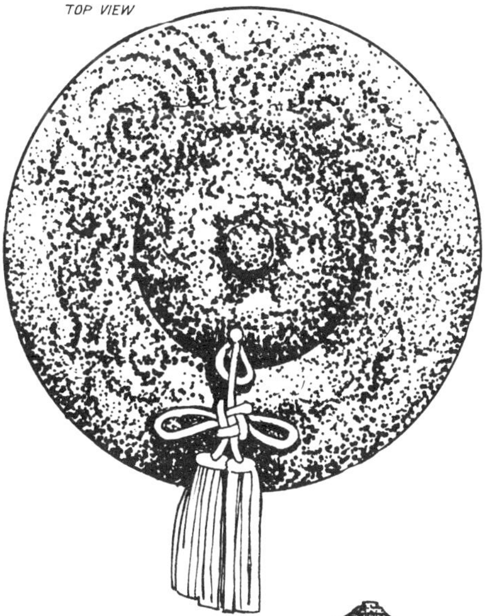

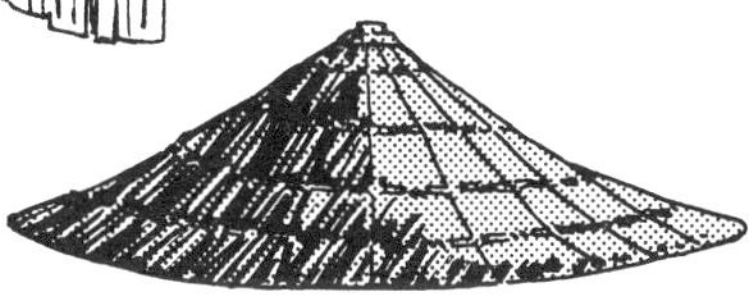

ARMOUR TYPE	CUT RF	CHOP RF	THRUST RF	IMPACT RF	DEX	MASS
Thin Cloth	1	0	0	0	0	1.3kg
Medium Cloth	2	0	0	0	0	2.5kg
Heavy Cloth	3	1	1	1	1	3.7kg
Soft Leather	2	1	1	1	1	3.7kg
Hard Leather	3	2	3	1	1	5kg
Quilt	3	1	2	2	1	5kg
Padded	4	1	2	3	1	5kg
Woven Cord	4	2	3	2	2	5kg
Heavy Cloth Ringmail	5	3	3	1	1	7.5kg
Soft Leather Ringmail	4	3	3	1	1	7.5kg
Hard Leather Ringmail	5	4	5	1	2	10kg
Quilt Ringmail	5	3	4	2	2	10kg
Studded Heavy Cloth	3	1	1	1	1	6kg
Studded Soft Leather	3	1	1	1	1	6kg
Studded Hard Leather	4	2	3	1	2	7.5kg
Hard Leather Jazeraint	7	6	4	1	2	10kg
Hard Wood Jazeraint	6	5	4	1	2	10kg
Horn/Bone Jazeraint	8	7	6	1	2	15kg
Metal Jazeraint	9	8	8	1	2	20kg
Mail	7	6	2	1	1	20kg
Combined Mail	8	7	5	1	2	22kg
Metal Brigandine	9	9	8	2	3	22kg
Laminated	9	9	9	1	2	20kg
Metal Lamellar	9	9	8	1	3	18kg
Plate	11	11	11	1	2	25kg

ARMOUR TYPE DESCRIPTIONS

Light Cloth is equivalent to linen.

Medium Cloth is equivalent to denim.

Heavy Cloth is equivalent to two or three thicknesses of medium cloth.

Soft Leather is equivalent to the outer covering of a modern day leather jacket.

Hard Leather is equal to approximately five millimeters of leather.

Quilt Armour consists of cotton or some other soft material which is sandwiched between two layers of cloth.

Padded Armour generally consists of felt or some other thick cloth about three to eight centimeters in thickness.

Woven Cord Armour resembles modern day macrame.

Ring Mail is simply metal rings which are sewn onto a suitable backing material (leather, cloth, etc.).

Studded Mail consists of metal studs attached to a backing cloth or leather.

Jazeraint Armour also known as Scale Armour, consists of scales of various sizes sewn or riveted onto a suitable backing.

Mail consists of small metal rings interconnected together to form a sort of fabric of metal.

Combined Mail consists of small pieces of metal interspaced with sections of normal mail.

Brigandine Armour consists of overlapping metal scales sandwiched between two layers of leather. The outer appearance of this armour resembles studded leather.

Laminated Armour consists of small metal strips which are overlapped and articulate upon each other.

Lamellar Armour, also known as Splint Armour, consists of small pieces of armour which are laced together. The size of the pieces depend on the portion of the body they are to protect.

Plate Armour consists of large pieces of metal which are either worn over other armour or attached to one another by a series of straps, buckles, or lacing.

GENERAL DESCRIPTION OF ARMOUR TYPES

In order to give a better understanding of the various types of armour used in the orient, the following is a brief description of each basic type. Each armour type is given a set of various numerical values. They are explained as follows:

Cut RF - A relative indication called Resistance Factor of how well the armour protects against cut attacks.

Chop RF - A relative indication of how resistant this type of armour is to chop attacks.

Thrust RF - A relative indication of how resistant this type of armour is to thrust attacks.

Impact RF - A relative indication of how resistant this type of armour is to impact attacks.

DEX - An indication of how much a suit of this armour would slow a character down. The higher this number the slower the character would move due to restricted flexability, higher mass, etc.

mass - The mass of a suit of this type of armour based on the wearer being 180cm (5'10") tall and 80kg (175lbs) in mass.

The main differences between a cut attack and a chop attack are the sharpness and curvature of the weapon's blade. If one general armour "class" is desired, the "chop" rating may be used.

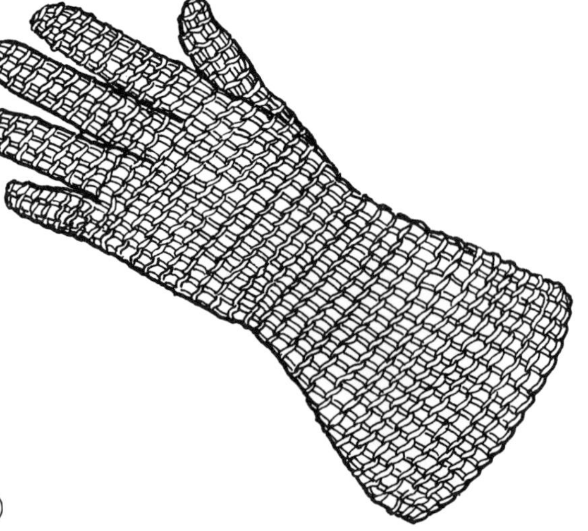

WARRIOR IN FULL ARMOUR (YOROI)

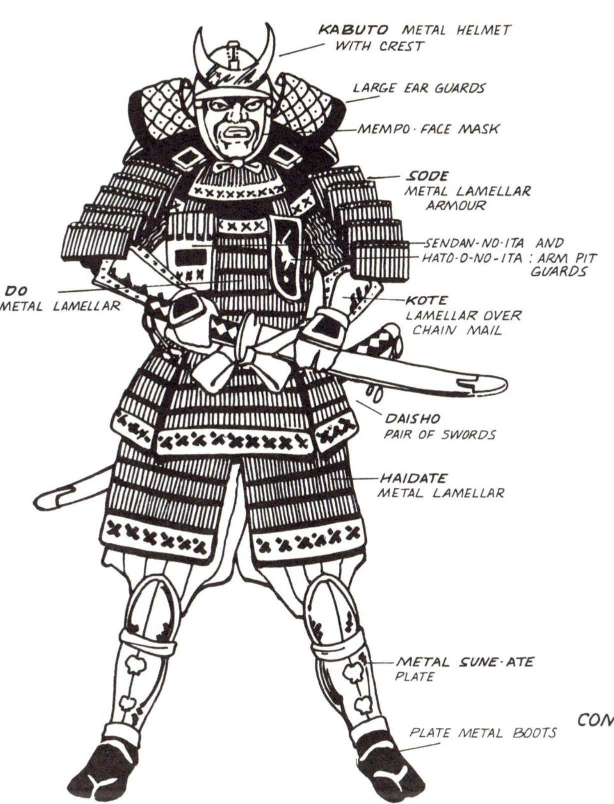

ARMOUR VALUES

ARMOUR VALUES

Type	Cut RF	Chop RF	Thrust RF	Impact RF
Plate	11	11	11	1
Metal Lamellar	9	9	8	1
Lamellar over Combined Mail (arms)	17	16	14	2
Mass: 20kg.				

COMMANDER IN FULL ARMOUR

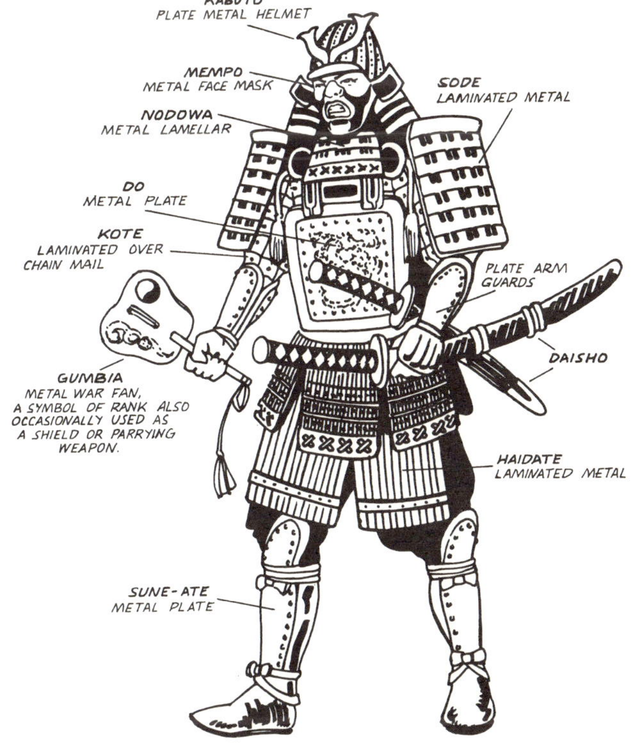

ARMOUR VALUES

Type	Cut RF	Chop RF	Thrust RF	Impact RF
Plate	11	11	11	1
Laminated	9	9	9	1
Laminated over Combined Mail (arms)	17	16	14	2
Mass: 21kg.				

For further information on these types of armour please refer to The Palladium Book of Weapons and Armour.

STEPS IN DONNING JAPANESE ARMOUR

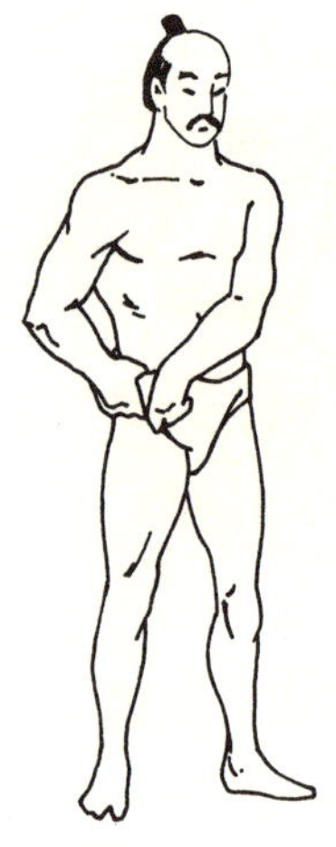

SHORT FUNDOSHI

SHITAGI AND OBI

KOBAKAMA

TABI SPLIT TOE BOOT

KYAHAN

WARAJI SANDALS

SUNE-ATE SHIN GUARDS

HAIDATE THIGH GUARDS

CHAIN MAIL SLEEVES

KOTE ARMOUR SLEEVES

WAKIBIKI

DO

UWA-OBI BELT

SODE SHOULDER GUARD

DAISHO WAKIZASHI AND KATANA SWORDS

NODOWA NECK GUARD AND HACHIMAKI

MEMPO FACE MASK AND KABUTO HELMET

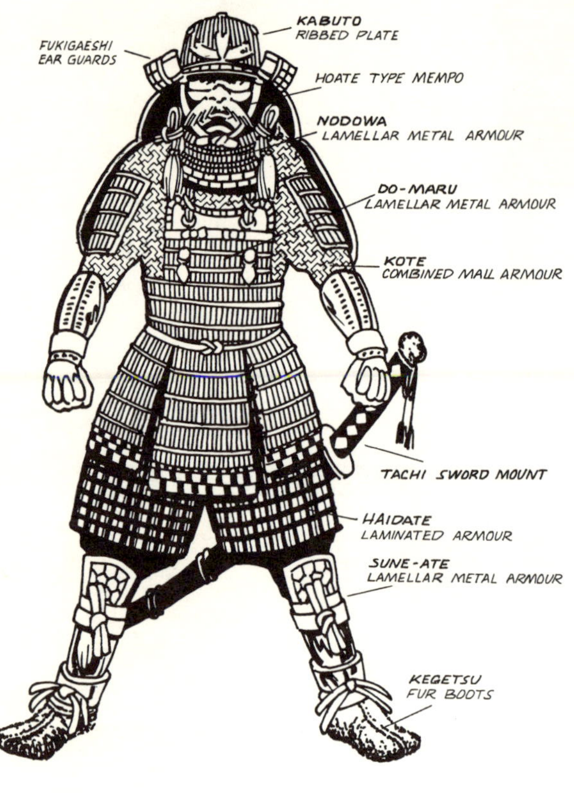

ARMOUR VALUES

Type	Cut RF	Chop RF	Thrust RF	Impact RF
Metal Lamellar	9	9	8	1
Laminated	9	9	9	1
Combined Mail	8	7	5	1
Ribbed Plate	12	12	12	1

ARMOUR VALUES

Type	Cut RF	Chop RF	Thrust RF	Impact RF
Laminated over Combined Mail	17	16	14	2
Mass 18kg.				

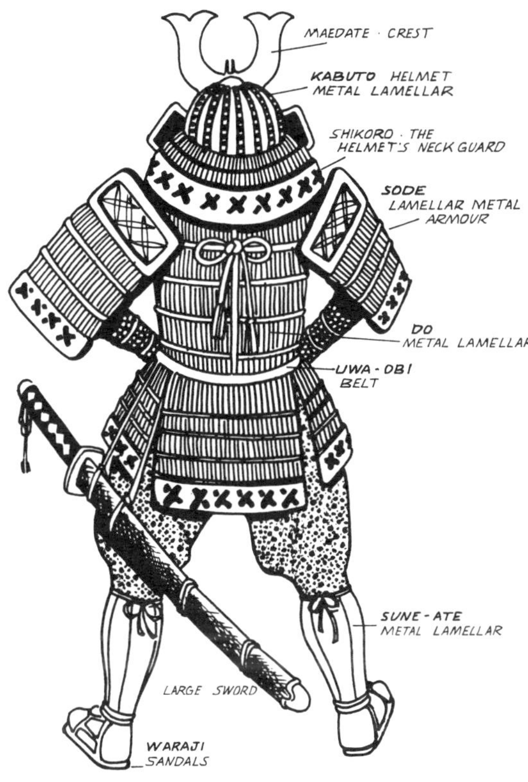

The Same Armour Values as Lamellar Combined.

EXAMPLES OF KOTE ARMOURED SLEEVES

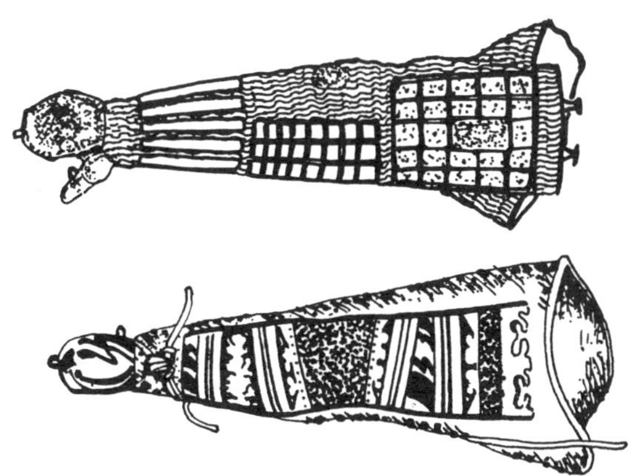

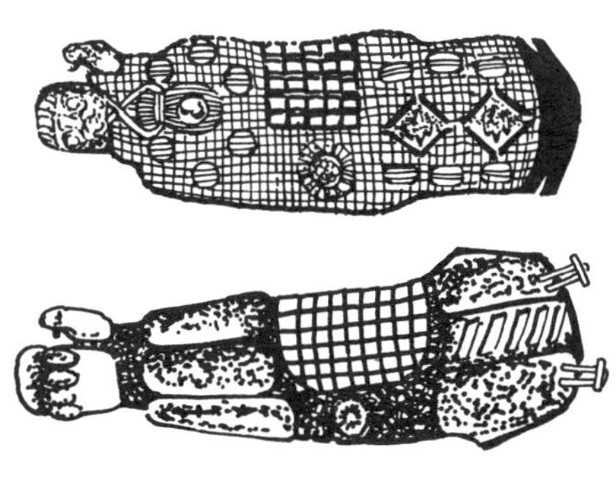

These pieces consist of mail interspaced with metal plates (combined mail). The mail is attached to a fabric backing to prevent chafing. The elbow, elbow joint, wrist, hand, and shoulder were typical areas of reinforcement.

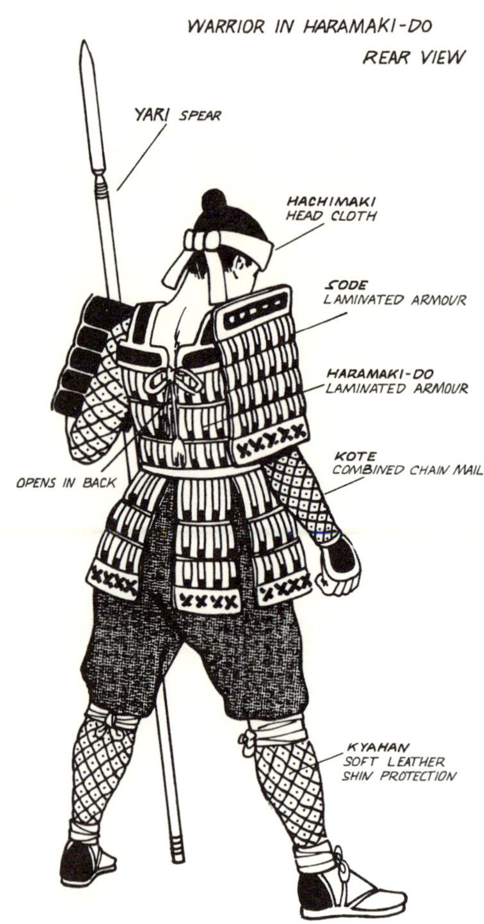

ARMOUR VALUES

Type	Cut RF	Chop RF	Thrust RF	Impact RF
Soft Leather	2	1	1	1
Combined Mail	8	7	5	1
Laminated (breast plate)	9	9	9	1
Laminated over combined Mail	17	16	14	2
Mass: 8kg.,				

WARRIOR IN HARAMAKI-DO

ARMOUR VALUES

Type	Cut RF	Chop RF	Thrust RF	Impact RF
Metal Lamellar	9	9	8	1
Combined Mail	8	7	5	1
Metal Jazeraint over Combined Mail	17	15	13	2
Mass: 10kg.				

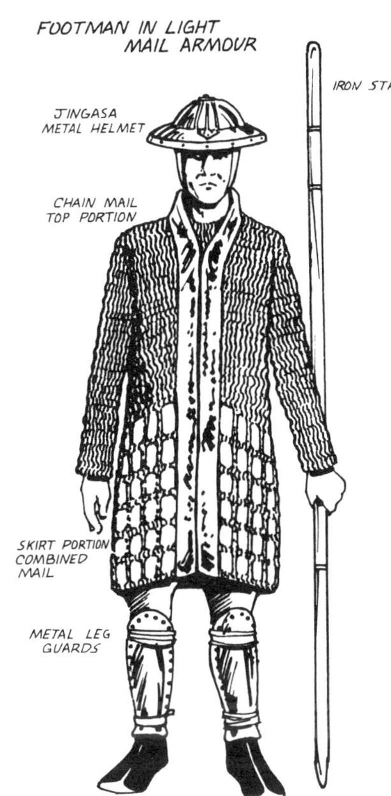

ARMOUR VALUES

Type	Cut RF	Chop RF	Thrust RF	Impact RF
Mail	7	6	2	1
Combined Mail	8	7	5	1
Mass: 9kg.,				

This armour could be worn under ordinary cloths for protection when on secret missions or when the impression of being unarmoured was important.

ARMOUR VALUES

Type	Cut RF	Chop RF	Thrust RF	Impact RF
Lamellar	9	9	8	1
Mass: 4kg.				

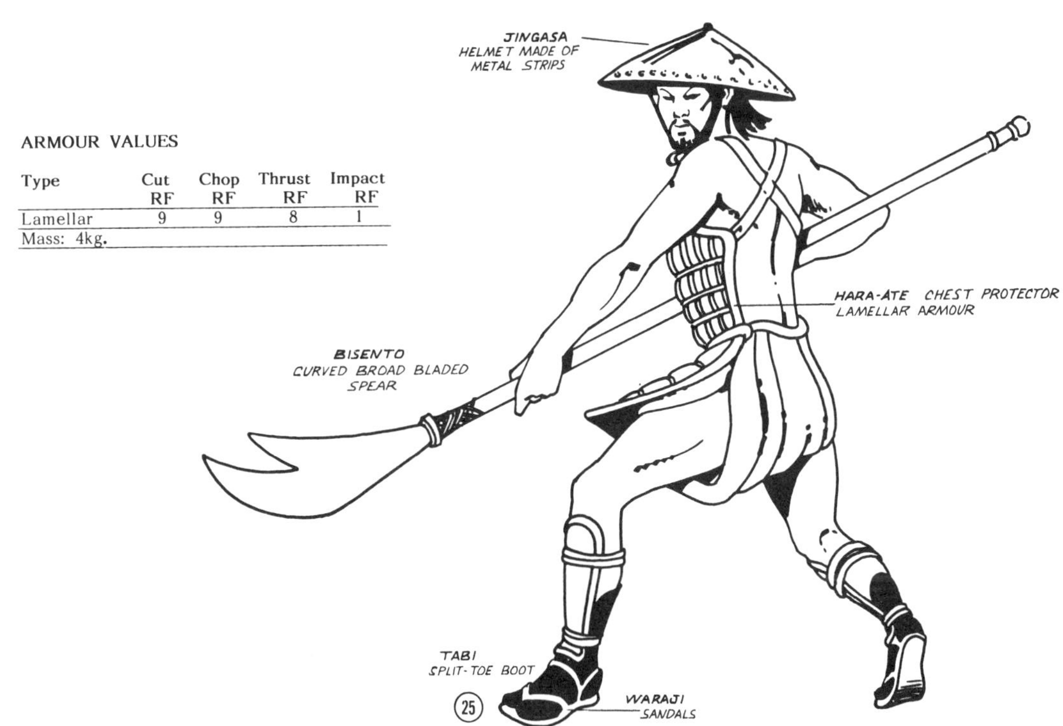

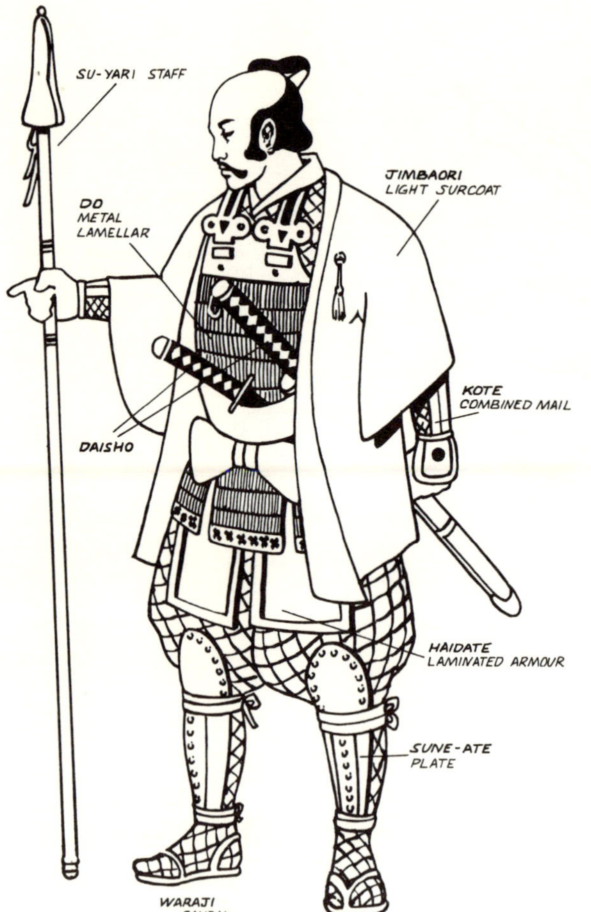

ARMOUR VALUES

Type	Cut RF	Chop RF	Thrust RF	Impact RF
Plate	11	11	11	1
Metal Lamellar	9	9	8	1
Laminated	9	9	9	1
Combined Mail	8	7	5	1

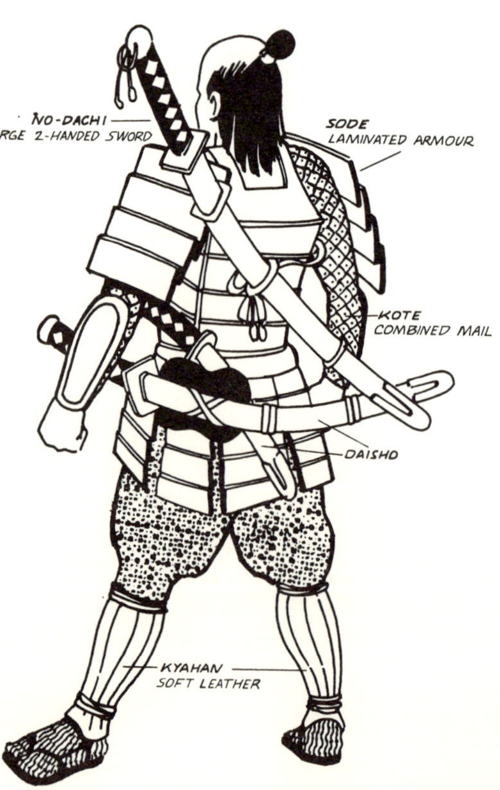

ARMOUR VALUES

Type	Cut RF	Chop RF	Thrust RF	Impact RF
Laminated	9	9	9	1
Combined Mail	8	7	5	1
Soft Leather	2	1	1	1

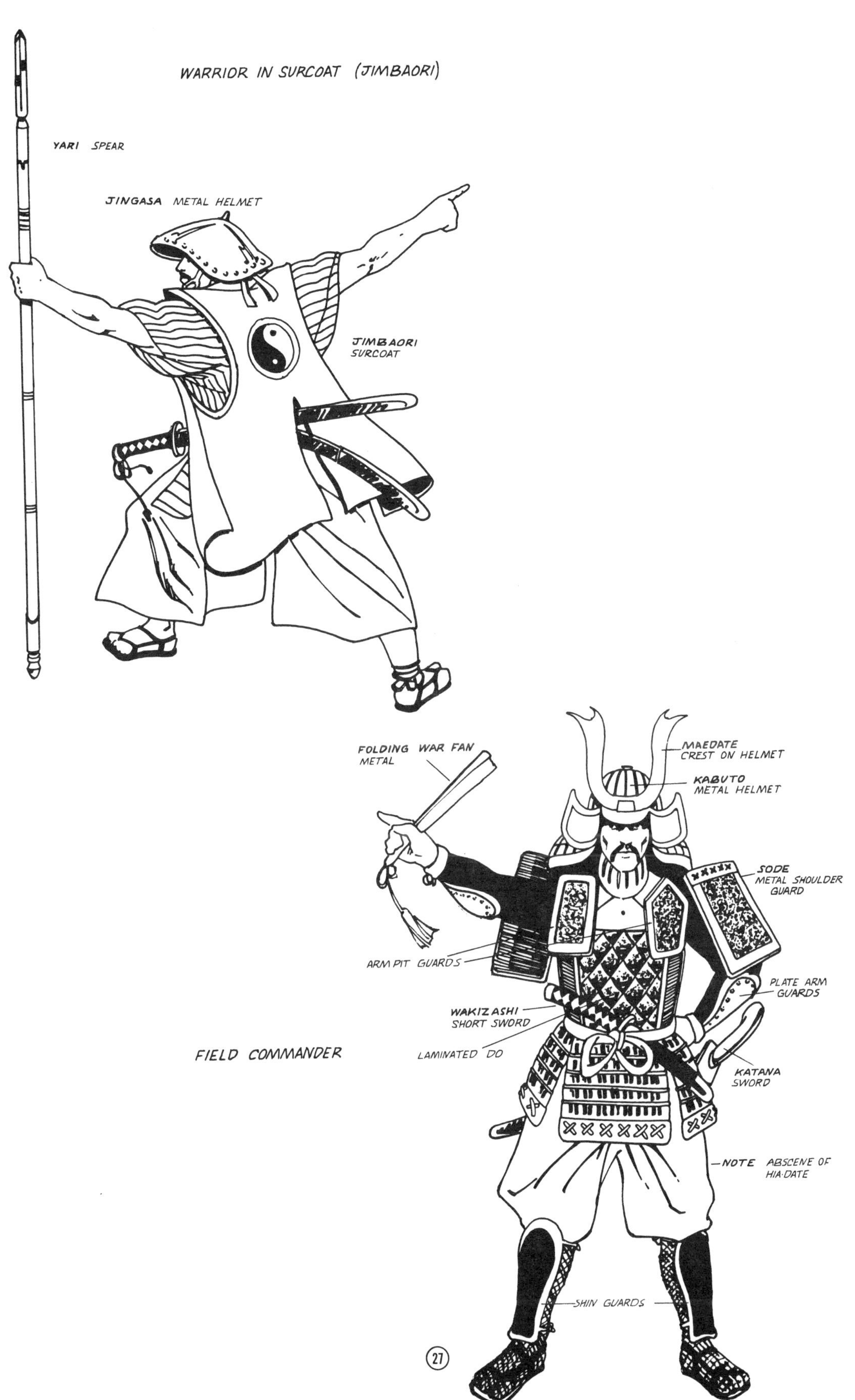
WARRIOR IN SURCOAT (JIMBAORI)
YARI SPEAR
JINGASA METAL HELMET
JIMBAORI
SURCOAT
FOLDING WAR FAN
METAL
MAEDATE
CREST ON HELMET
KABUTO
METAL HELMET
SODE
METAL SHOULDER
GUARD
ARM PIT GUARDS
PLATE ARM
GUARDS
WAKIZASHI
SHORT SWORD
FIELD COMMANDER
LAMINATED DO
KATANA
SWORD
NOTE ABSCENE OF
HIA·DATE
SHIN GUARDS

CHINESE ARMOUR

The armour of the Chinese remained relatively unchanged throughout the course of the ages. The Chinese employed various forms of padded ring, scale, and brigandine armour. Their best suits are of brigandine, which consists of two pieces of cloth with small metal plates between them. Important points on the body, such as the chest and knees, were frequently reinforced by metal plates.

Chinese helmets were made of steel and had brigandine neck guards attached to them.

In some instances armour consisted only of padding which was fitted with a number of gilt rivets. In this form the suit resembled brigandine but was actually much less encumbering in addition to being less protective.

The Chinese also used armour which appeared to be an ordinary garment, such as a shirt or jacket, but actually had overlapping metal plates attached to the inside.

Like most cultures, the Chinese had a number of pieces of armour which could be added or deleted depending upon the degree of protection wanted. Large shoulder guards of metal and leather could be worn. Shirts of brigandine could be added when fighting on foot. Forearm guards of laminated metal were also used.

ARMOUR VALUES

Type	Cut RF	Chop RF	Thrust RF	Impact RF
Metal Brigandine	9	9	8	2
Laminated	9	9	9	1
Double Layer Brigandine (Shoulder Area)	18	18	16	4
Mass: 22kg.				

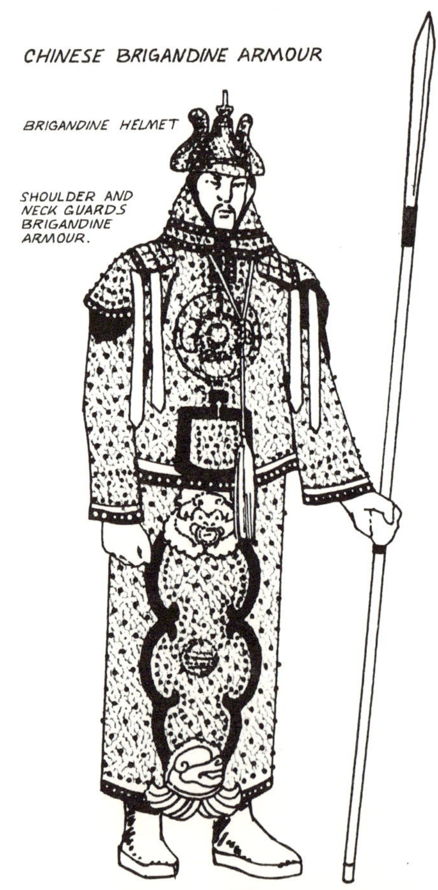

ARMOUR VALUES

Type	Cut RF	Chop RF	Thrust RF	Impact RF
Cloth Studded	3	1	1	1
Brigandine over Studded Cloth	12	10	9	3
Mass: 6kg.				

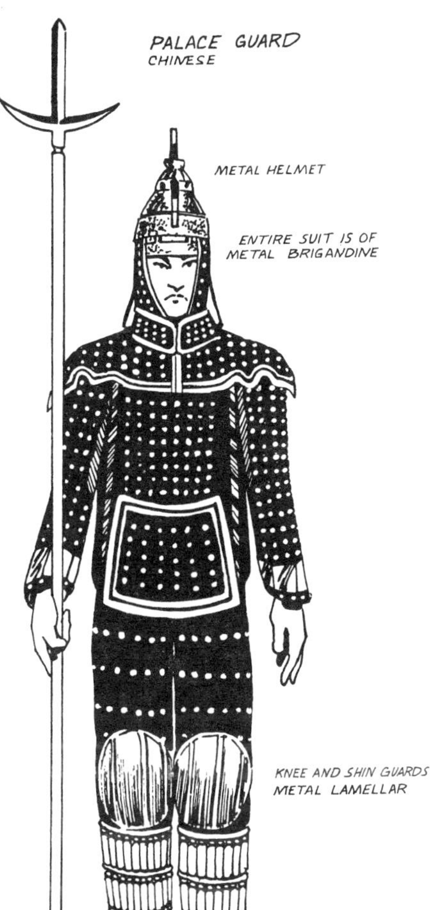

ARMOUR VALUES

Type	Cut RF	Chop RF	Thrust RF	Impact RF
Metal Brigandine	9	9	8	2
Mass: 22kg.				

ARMOUR VALUES

Type	Cut RF	Chop RF	Thrust RF	Impact RF
Metal Jazeraint	9	9	8	1
Mass: 18kg.				

CHINESE LIGHT ARMOUR

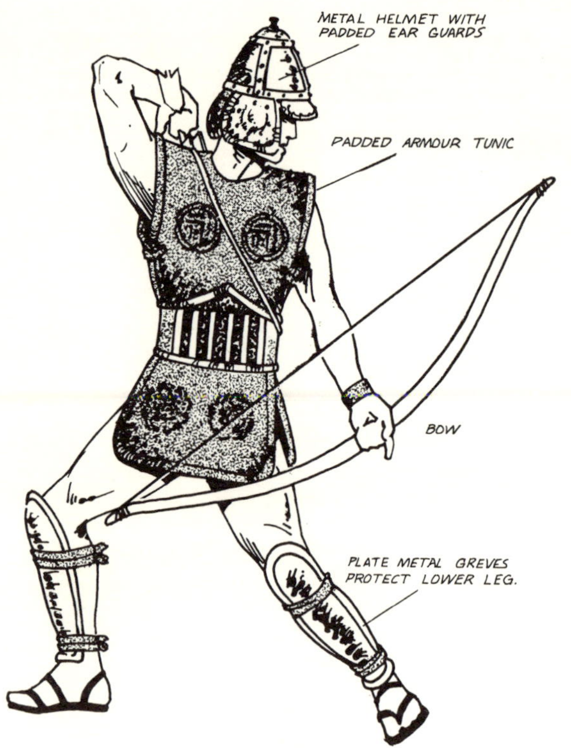

ARMOUR VALUES

Type	Cut RF	Chop RF	Thrust RF	Impact RF
Padded	4	1	2	3
Plate	11	11	11	11
Mass: 5kg.				

KOREAN ARMOUR

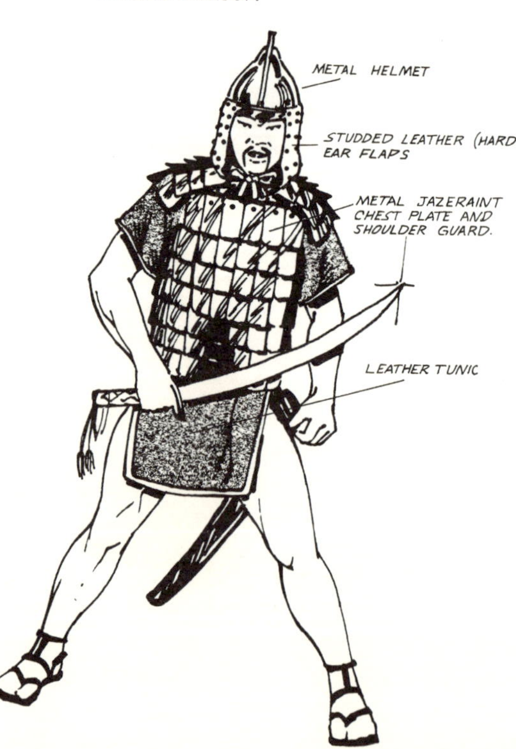

KOREAN ARMOUR

Korean armour was generally similar in construction to that of the Chinese. Wealthy warriors often were adorned in suits which were very elaborately decorated. The lower classes often wore heavily padded body armour up to four centimeters thick, which left the arms and legs bare. Hardened leather jazeraint coats were also worn.

In periods of conflict with Japan, a number of Japanese armours were also worn.

ARMOUR VALUES

Type	Cut RF	Chop RF	Thrust RF	Impact RF
Metal Jazeraint	9	9	8	1
St udded Hard Leather	4	2	3	1
Plate	11	11	11	1
Mass: 9kg.				

MALAYAN ARMOUR

In general, these people wore little or no armour. Some wore simple hides hanging down in front and back as protection from blowpipe darts. The Moros of the Phillippines wore armour made of hides, woven cord, or wooden scales. Armour made of brass or horn plates connected together by brass mail was also used, but these were rare and expensive.

ARMOUR VALUES

Type	Cut RF	Chop RF	Thrust RF	Impact RF
Bark Jazeraint	6	5	4	1
Mass: 4kg.				

ARMOUR VALUES

Type	Cut RF	Chop RF	Thrust RF	Impact RF
Hide (Hard Leather)	3	2	3	1
Padded	4	1	2	3
Mass: 2kg.				

CASTLES

JAPAN

JAPANESE FORTIFICATIONS

Japanese fortresses were generally built on top of mountains. The castle was either put atop a flat topped mountain or a leveled area near the top of the mountain. The castle site was then protected by large stone walls. Towards the end of the sixteenth century towers, or donjons, were added as well. These mountain castles, or **yamajiro,** were extremely difficult to attack.

Because the only effective means of taking a castle of this sort was by siege, there were additional buildings for the storage of weapons and food in the event of an attack. Often the **donjon** had a well for water and a kitchen for preparing food.

It was not too common for there to be a large enough town near these mountain castles to support the garrison. For this reason small towns sprang up at the foot of the castle's mountain. These towns were inhabited by the troops and their families, as well as the various merchants, shop-keepers, etc., which catered to them. These castle towns were called **johamachi.**

The rough terrain which was good for defensive purposes was generally not suitable for the development of towns however. For this reason castles began to be situated on hills in the middle of the warlord's **(daimyo)** territory. There were called **hirayamajiro.**

Later, when wars became less and less frequent, the castle became more a political center from which to rule than a military base. The castle was now a symbol of authority and power. Castles were now built in open areas, wherever the political and economic life of the province was concentrated. These flatland castles were called **hirajiro.**

In general, the Japanese warrior did not plan to fight from withing the confines of the castle; he thought that fighting from outside the castle to be the best defense. Many daimyos were even unwilling to fight within the castle itself. If their compounds were successfully entered by attacking troops, they usually chose to die honorably by their own hand. The donjon was usually the site of ritual suicide if the defense was unsuccessful.

The buildings on a castle site were arrainged so that it would be difficult for an attacker to storm the site. At the heart of the whole structure was the main compound **(the hommaru compound)** which contained the donjon and the daimyo's residense. Subsidiary compounds were added on around the main compound. Stone walls and moats were placed around these compounds either in a concentric or spiral pattern so that the whole area was protected. Turrets were built on the walls with the largest being on the corners. The strong fortified outer walls were built of stones with a steep slope.

Inside the compound, the pathways to the donjon often took on a maze-like appearance. Unexpected turns, dead ends, and gates would impede the attack while the defenders could fire arrows or drop stones down from the walls.

Often the town outside the castle was also laid out so that there was no clear-cut path to the gates. Blind alleys and unexpected obstructions would impede any advance. In general the towns around the castles were inhabited by many of the diamyo's warriors.

THE MAJOR COMPONENTS OF JAPANESE CASTLES

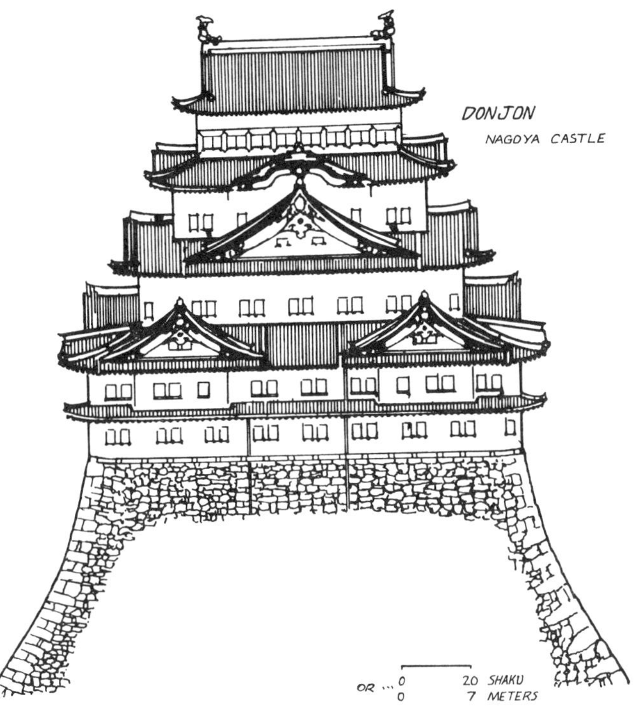

DONJON
NAGOYA CASTLE

GATE TYPES

INSET GATE

TURRET GATE
AS FOUND AT HIMEJI CASTLE

KORAI GATE

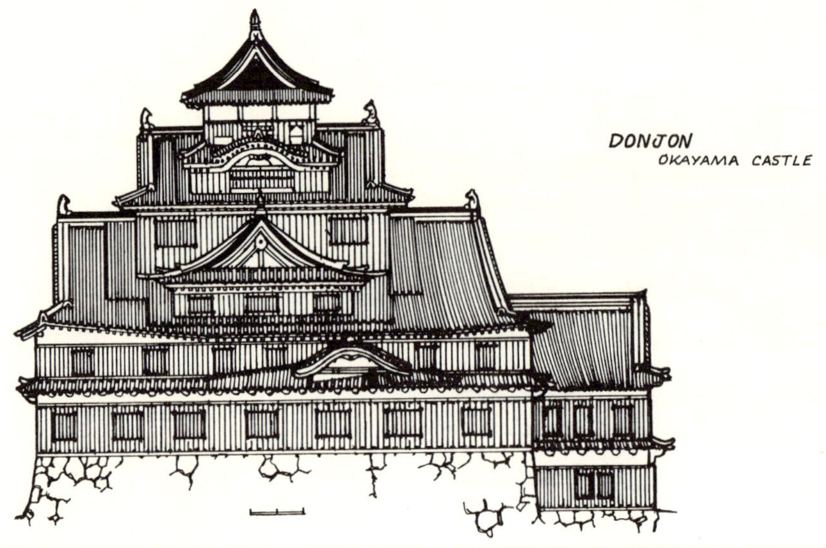

DONJON
OKAYAMA CASTLE

TYPES OF STONE WALLS

COMPACT

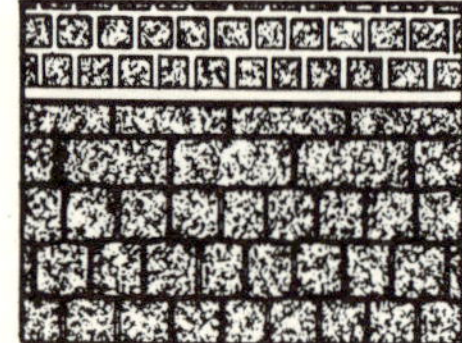

RANDOM

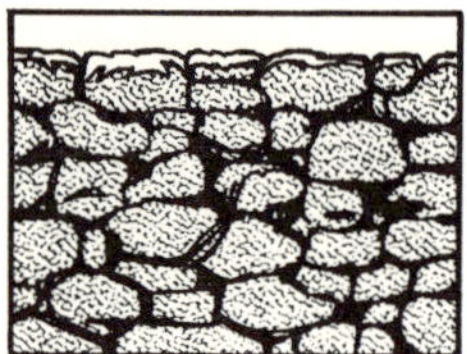

PATCHY

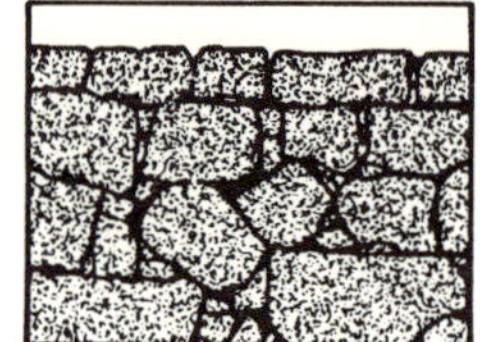

STONE DROPPING PROJECTION

PARTS OF A DONJON
CASTLE TOWER

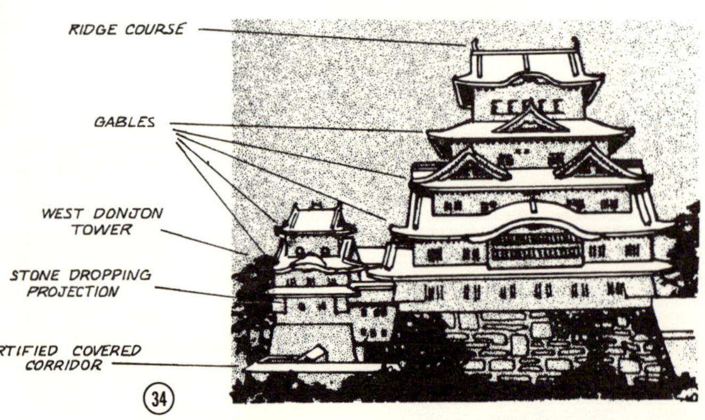

HIMEJI CASTLE

SUPPORT PILLARS FOR WALLS
MAIN ENTRANCE TO
THE DONJON

GROUND PLAN OF
DONJON OF MARUOKA
Ca. 1576

RIDGE COURSE
BALCONY
GABLES
ENTRANCE

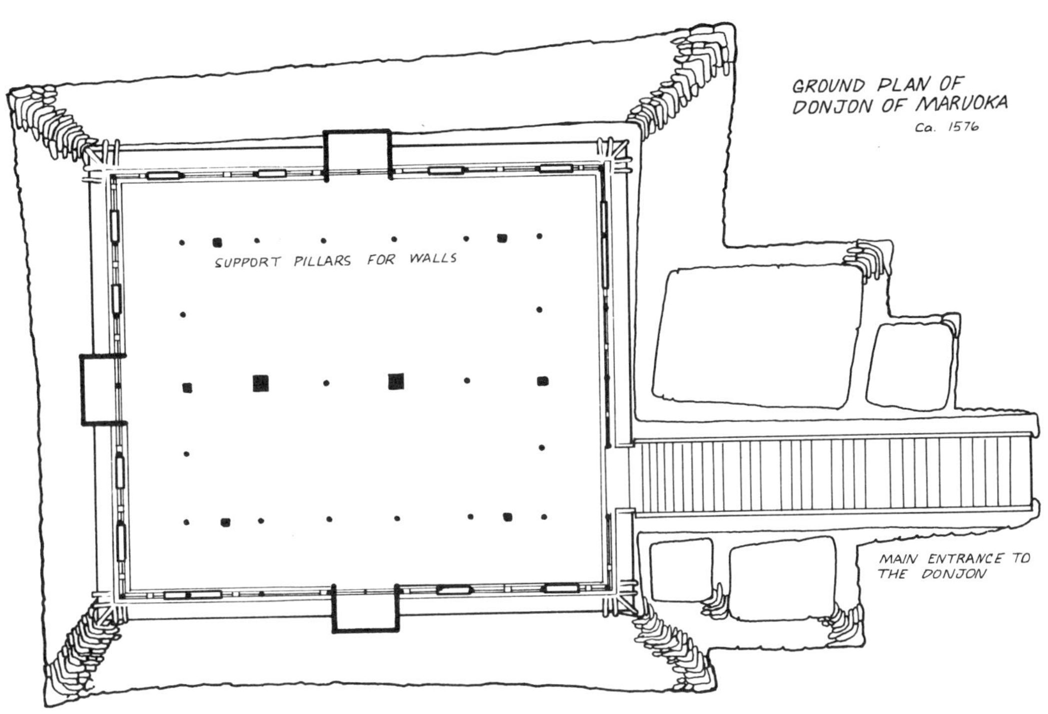

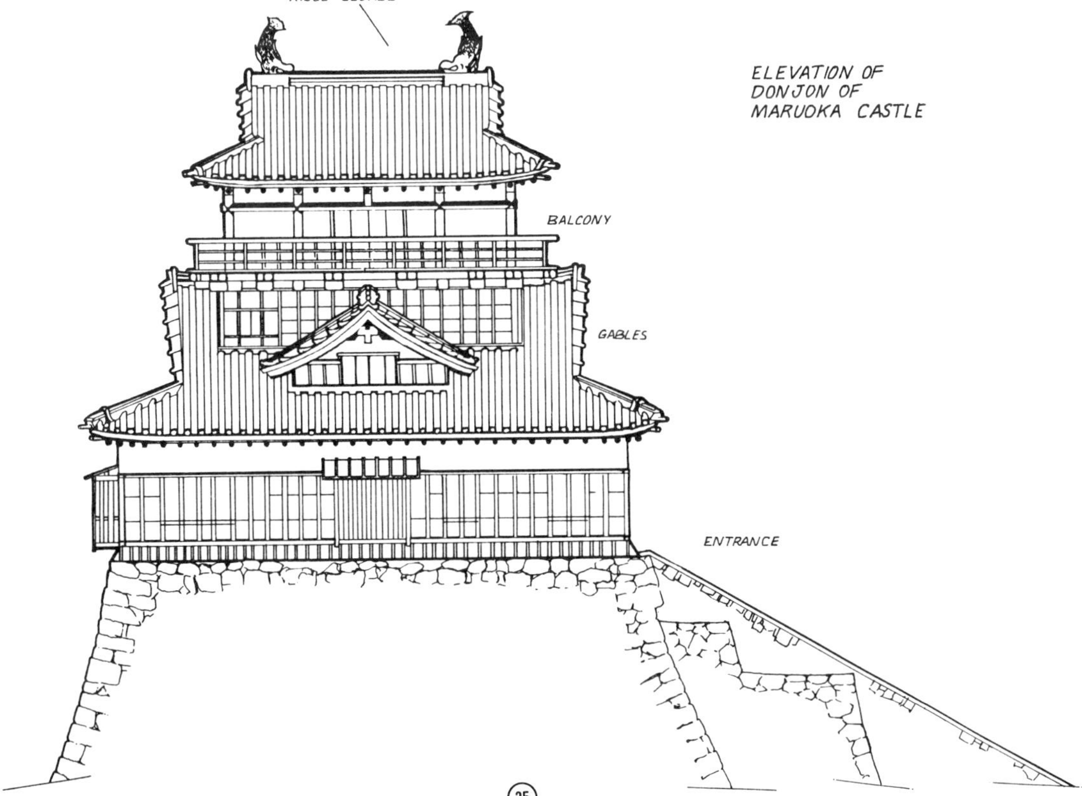

ELEVATION OF
DONJON OF
MARUOKA CASTLE

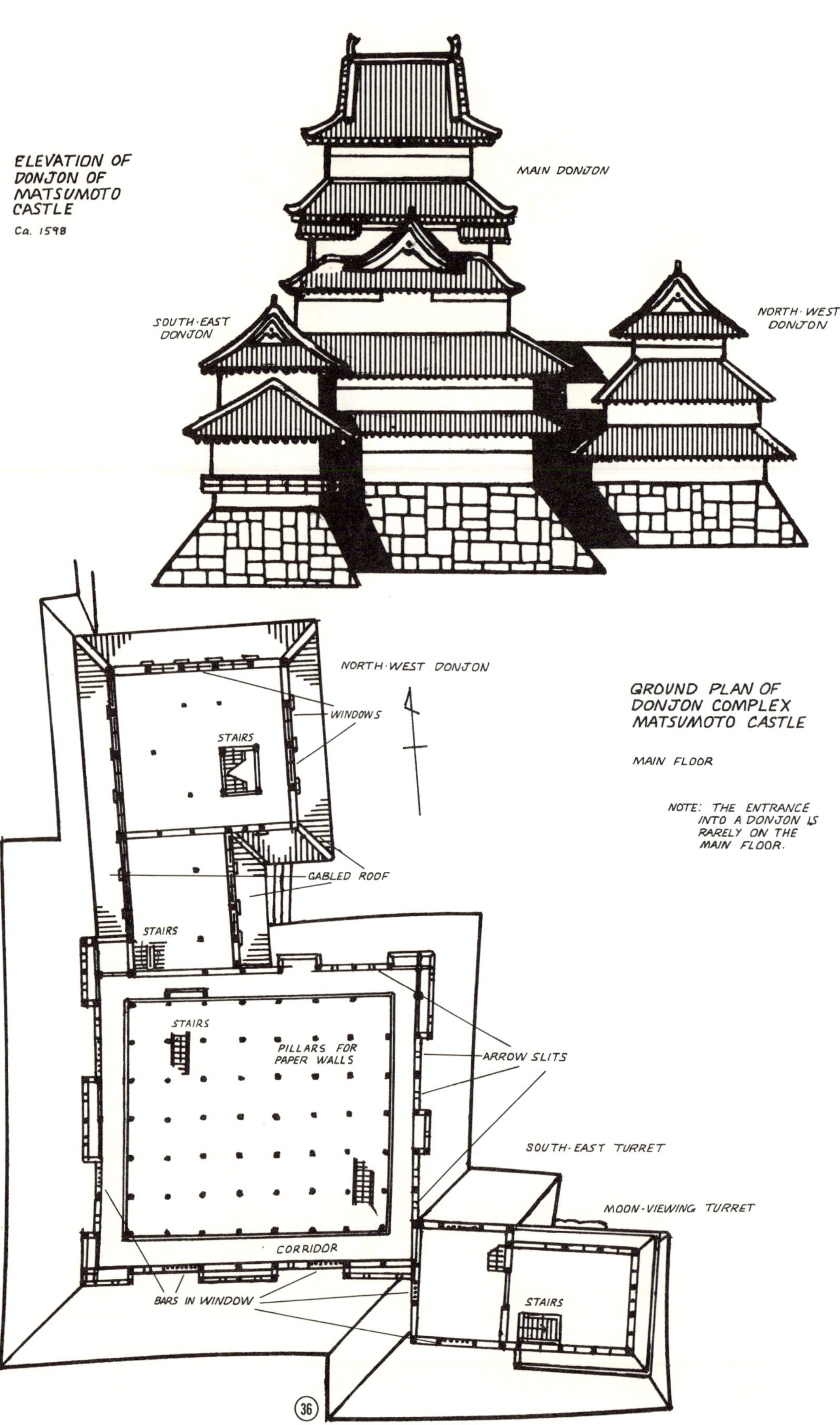
ELEVATION OF
DONJON OF
MATSUMOTO
CASTLE
Ca. 1598
MAIN DONJON
SOUTH·EAST
DONJON
NORTH·WEST
DONJON
NORTH·WEST DONJON
GROUND PLAN OF
DONJON COMPLEX
MATSUMOTO CASTLE
MAIN FLOOR
NOTE: THE ENTRANCE
INTO A DONJON IS
RARELY ON THE
MAIN FLOOR.
WINDOWS
STAIRS
GABLED ROOF
STAIRS
STAIRS
PILLARS FOR
PAPER WALLS
ARROW SLITS
SOUTH·EAST TURRET
MOON-VIEWING TURRET
CORRIDOR
STAIRS
BARS IN WINDOW

OSAKA CASTLE PLAN

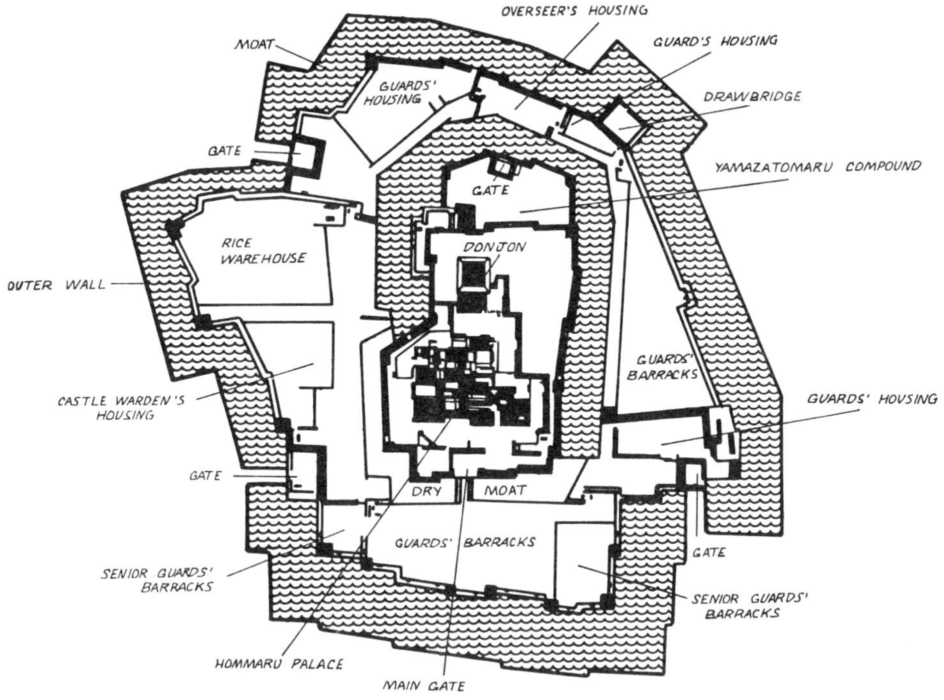

OSAKA CASTLE AS DEPICTED IN THE 17th CENTURY

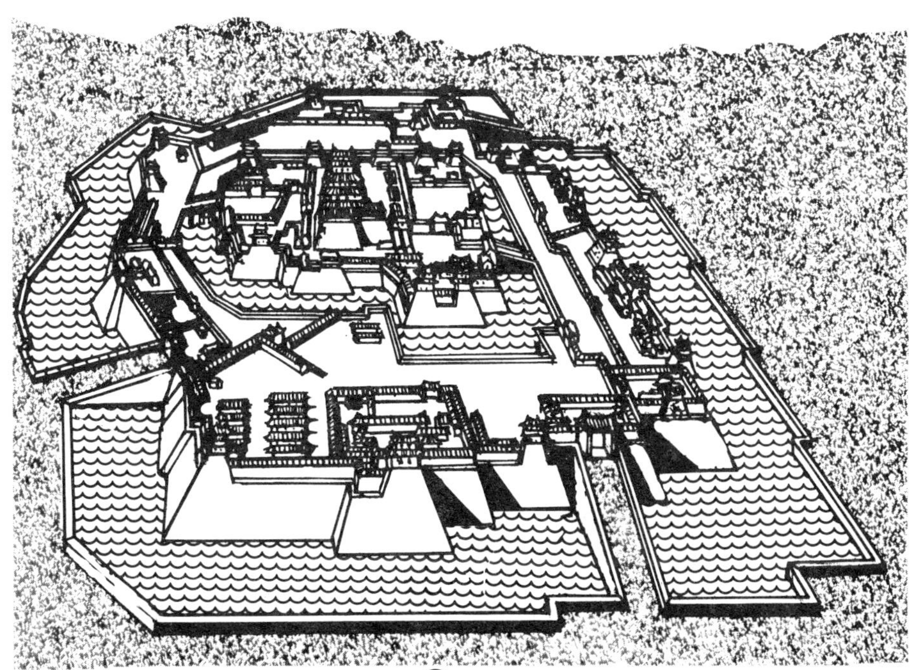

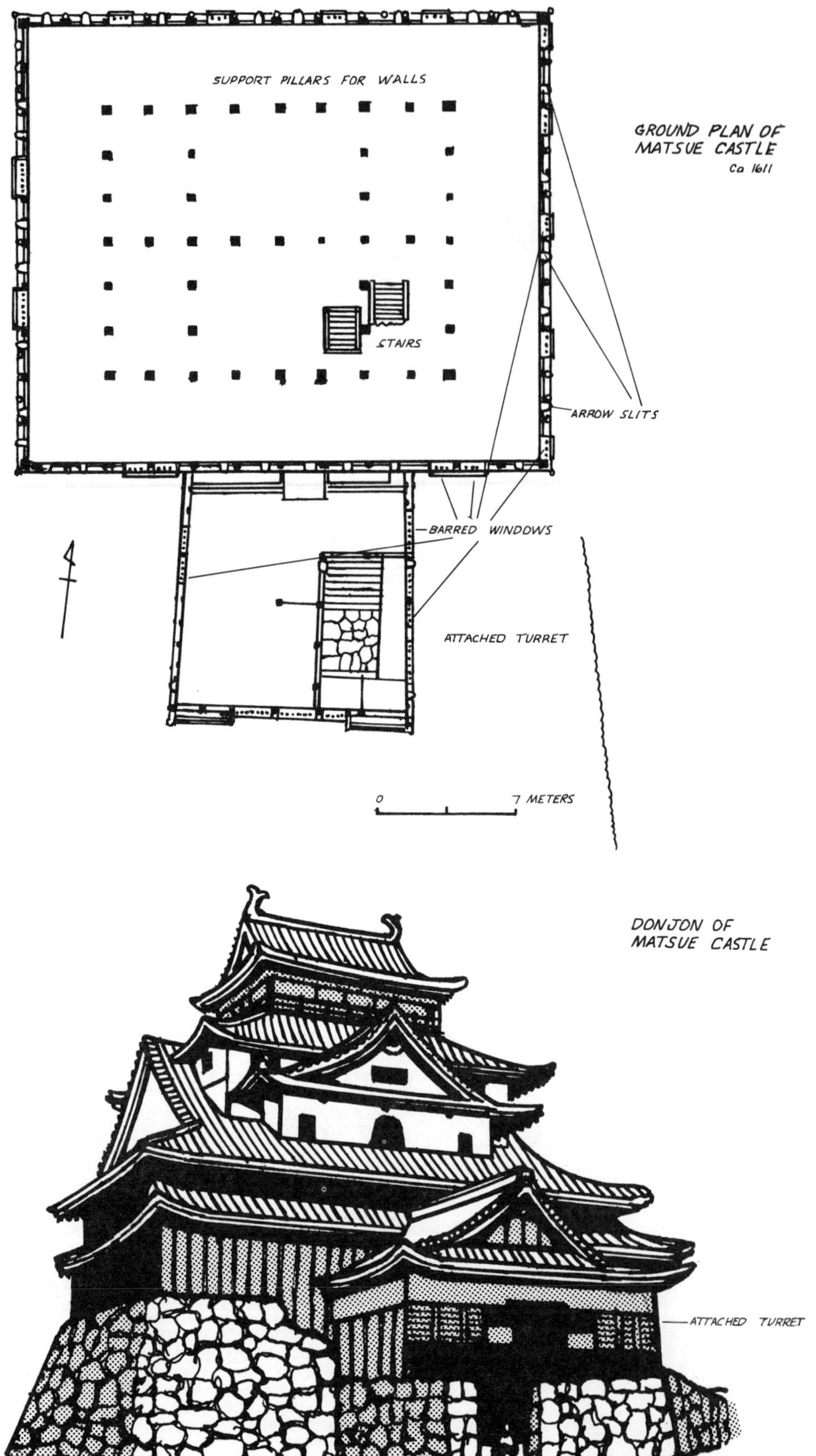
SUPPORT PILLARS FOR WALLS
GROUND PLAN OF
MATSUE CASTLE
Ca 1611
STAIRS
ARROW SLITS
BARRED WINDOWS
ATTACHED TURRET
0
7 METERS
DONJON OF
MATSUE CASTLE
ATTACHED TURRET
PERSON AT GATE·WAY TO INDICATE SCALE

GENERAL GROUND PLAN OF HIMEJI CASTLE AND SURROUNDING TOWN.

HIMEJI DONJON · FRONT VIEW

MOAT

TOWNSPEOPLES' DISTRICT

WARRIORS' DISTRICT

TEMPLES AND SHRINES

HIMEJI CASTLE GROUND

HOMMARU COMPOUND

NINOMARU COMPOUND

NISHINOMARU COMPOUND

SANNOMARU COMPOUND

WEST RESIDENCE

EAST-SIDE VIEW OF HIMEJI CASTLE

HIMEJI CASTLE GROUND PLAN

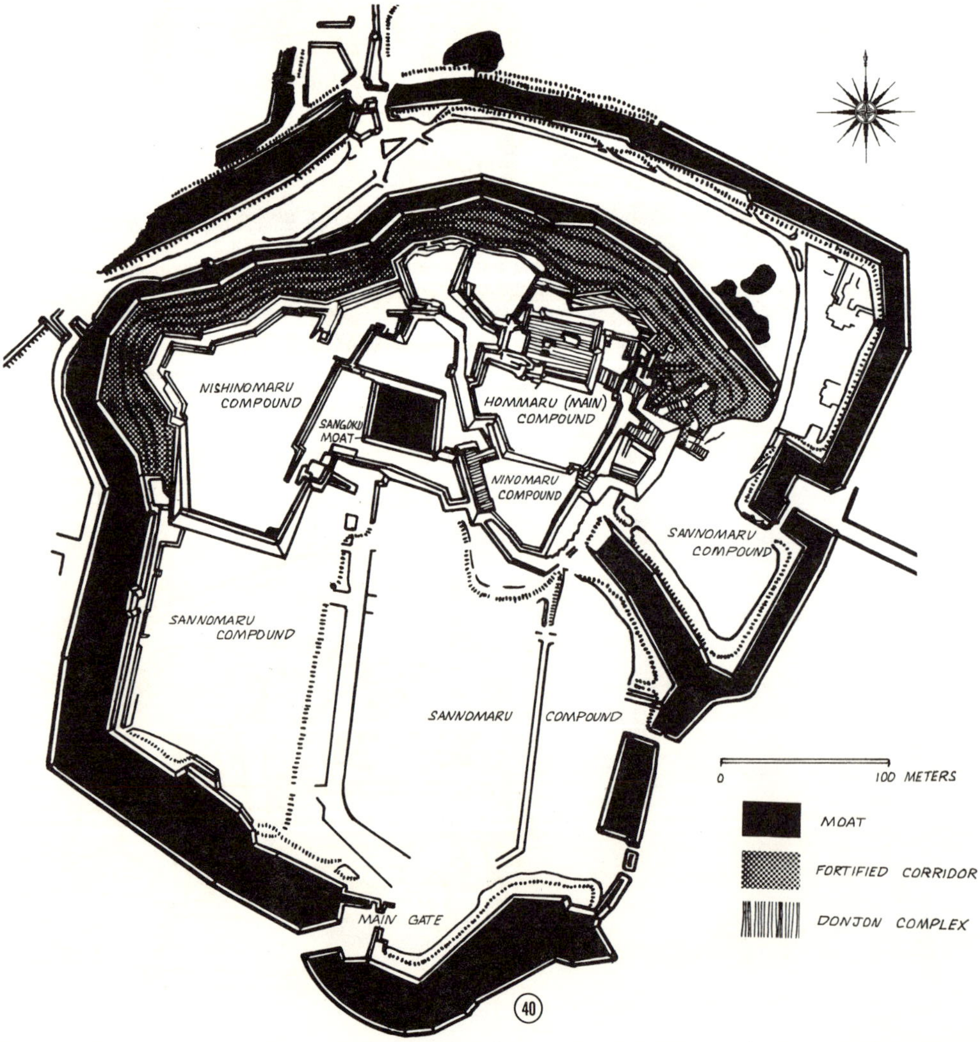

NISHINOMARU COMPOUND

SANGOKU MOAT

HOMMARU (MAIN) COMPOUND

NINOMARU COMPOUND

SANNOMARU COMPOUND

SANNOMARU COMPOUND

SANNOMARU COMPOUND

MAIN GATE

0 100 METERS

MOAT

FORTIFIED CORRIDOR

DONJON COMPLEX

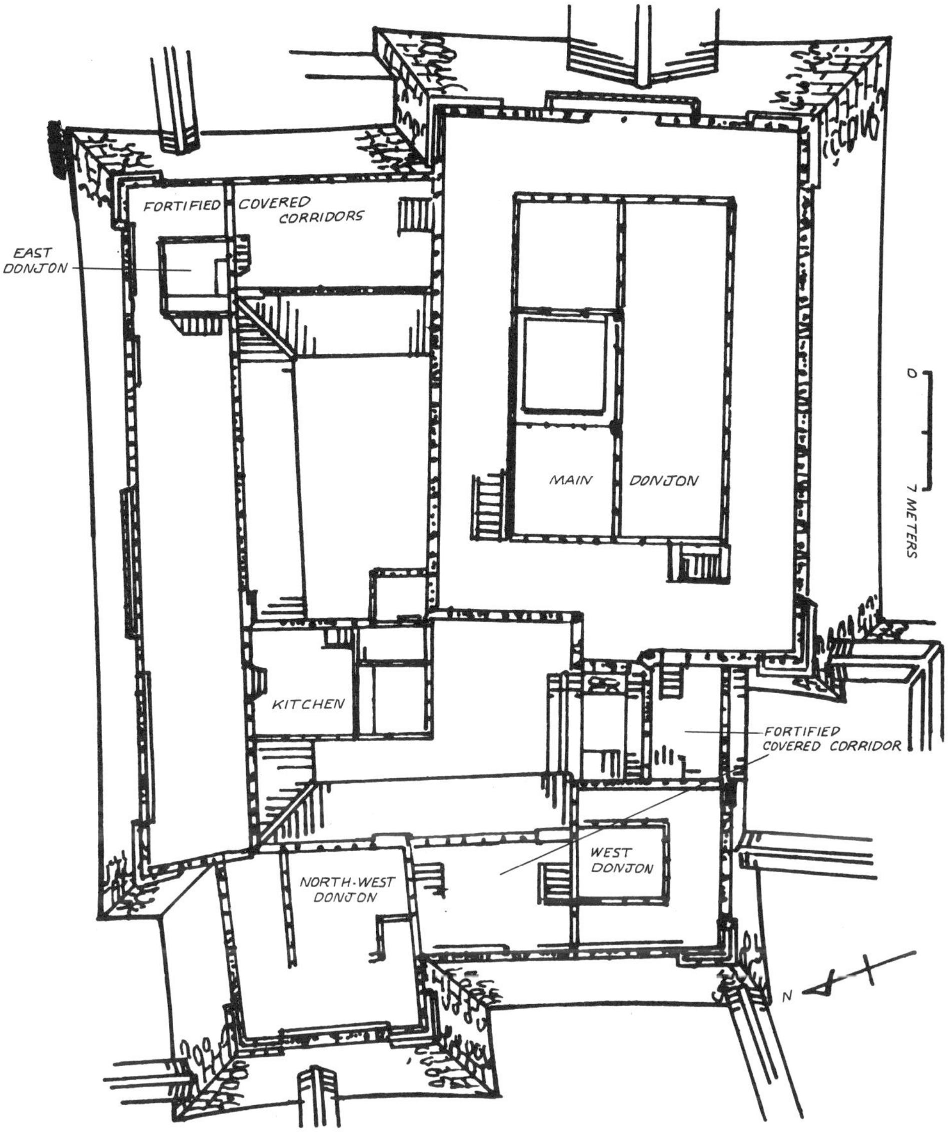

FORTIFIED COVERED CORRIDORS

EAST DONJON

MAIN DONJON

0

7 METERS

KITCHEN

FORTIFIED COVERED CORRIDOR

WEST DONJON

NORTH-WEST DONJON

N

GROUND PLAN OF DONJON COMPLEX OF HIMEJI CASTLE
Ca. 1609

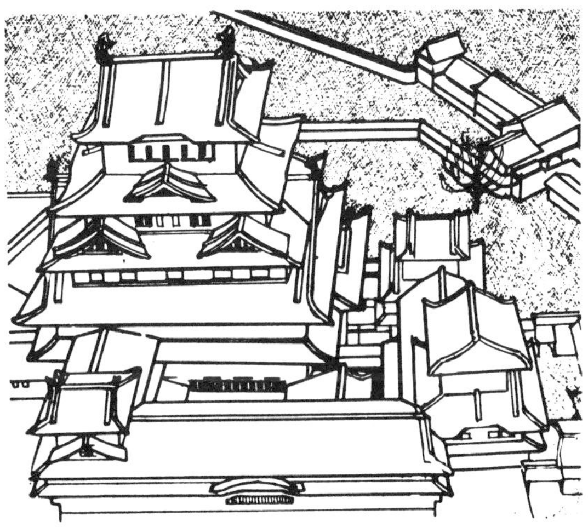

VIEW OF THE GREAT WALL OF CHINA

CHINA

CHINESE FORTIFICATIONS

In China the majority of the major cities were heavily fortified by walls and towers, some of which make the largest European castles seem insignificant. Although many of these fortifications have been dated to the Ming Dynasty (1368-1644) they were certainly only a renewal of prior constructions. In general, the walls are built of brick which is laid down in many courses. The base of the wall was frequently strengthened by a plith of stone. Often large towers are placed along the walls to aid in defense.

The base of these walls were often from 15 to 25 meters thick. They rose to great heights, up to 25 meters, and were topped by crenellated ramparts. Gateways through the walls are usually made of heavy timbers. In contrast to the immense walls these doors seem very weak. To counter this large gatehouses were built which as Marco Polo related in the end of the thirteenth century, could hold up to one-thousand men.

THE GREAT WALL OF CHINA

Perhaps the most famous example of defensive fortification is what is known as **The Great Wall of China**. It can safely be said that this massive piece of architecture outshines almost every other single structure built by human hands.

The Great Wall was not simply put up overnight. When the country was united at the onset of the Chhin Dynasty (221-207 B.C.), emperor Shih Huang Ti was intent upon stabilizing the territory by keeping the nomadic huns out. Actual construction began around 217 B.C. and utilized to a large extent, earlier existing ramparts which had been built in the earlier provinces. As the wall exists today, it is estimated to cover 3930 miles (6325 kilometers) with all of the various side-branches figured in. Many of the various loops and offshoots were constructed in subsequent centuries after the original line was built.

The wall achieved its purpose of keeping out the nomads by restricting the number which could pass this border. By eliminating the tactic of large numbers of horsemen sweeping down out of the steppes and sacking cities and towns, the nomadic tribesmen were eliminated as a major threat. If a large concentrated attack was made to capture a section of the wall or knock a breach in it, enough time could be bought by the defenders to enable reinforcements to arrive. The wall was much like a breakwater against which waves of nomads were broken and contained. It is theorized that the wall "channelled" the nomadic tribesmen to the west and into Europe.

Naturally the wall had its ups and downs. After the Chhin and Han Dynasties (3rd. century B.C. to 3rd century A.D.), there was little upkeep and maintenance. During the Wei, Chhi, and Sui Periods there was a major renovation and reconstruction (6th. and 7th. centuries A.D.). However, after this, again numerous centuries passed with no upkeep.

In general the wall was built upon a granite block base. The walls themselves were constructed of brick or stone with cores of rubble. There are usually eight to twelve towers per mile anywhere from 100 to 200 yards apart.

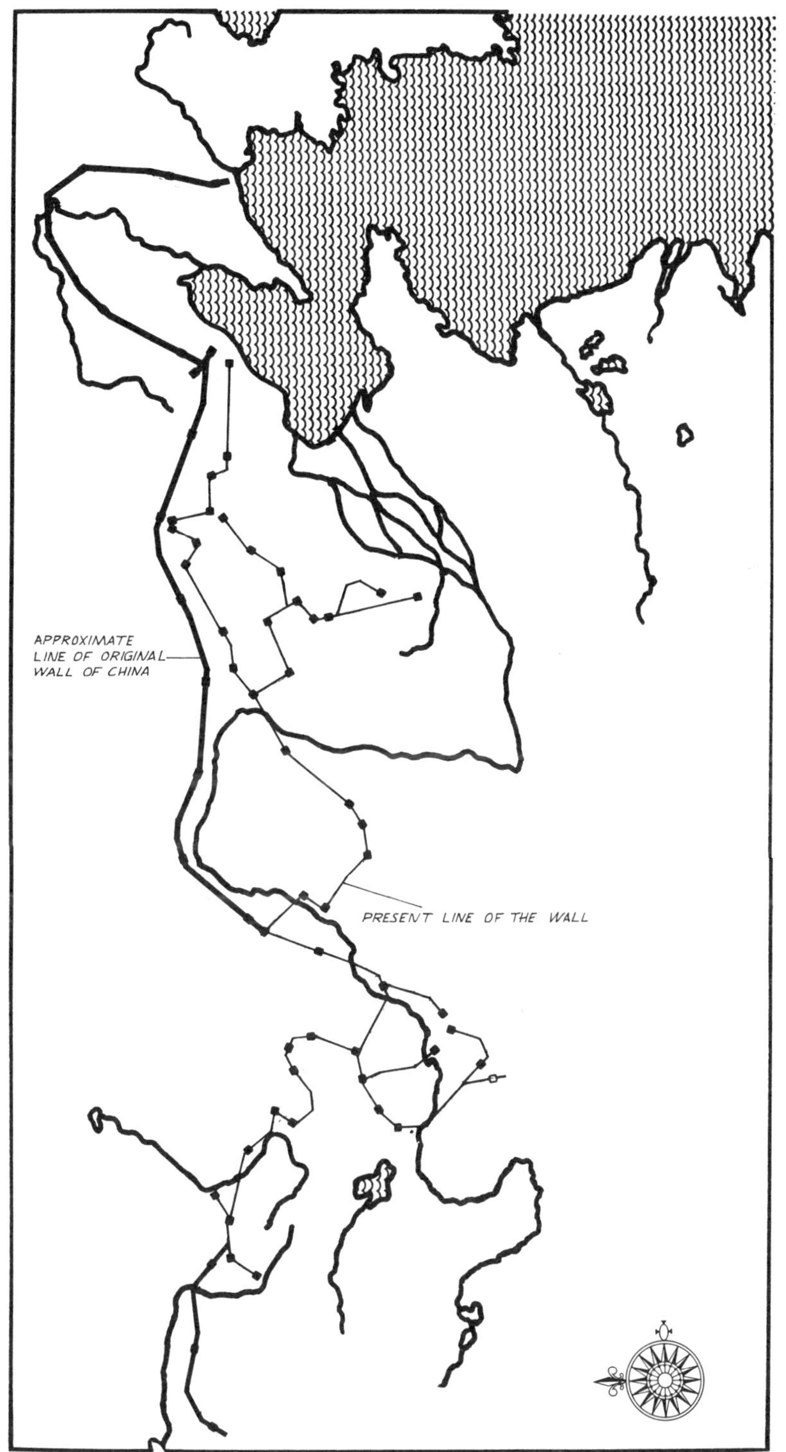

MAP OF NORTHERN CHINA SHOWING THE EX⁻ENT OF THE GREAT WALL

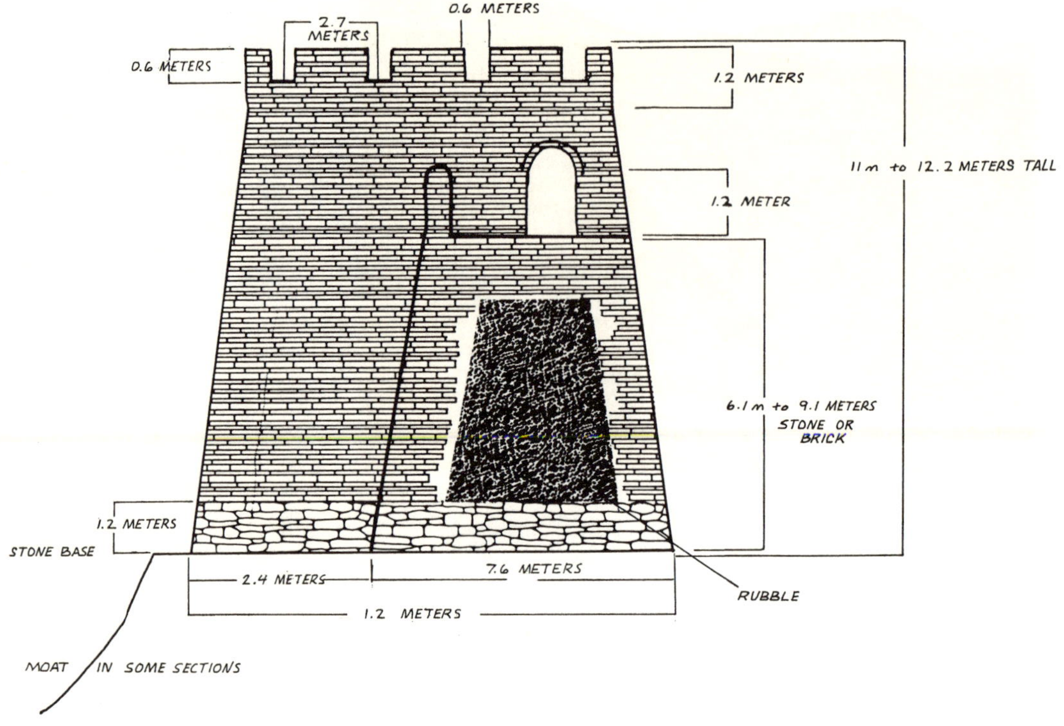

CROSS SECTION OF THE GREAT WALL

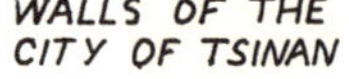

WALLS OF THE
CITY OF TSINAN

HEIGHT APPROXIMATELY
10 METERS (32 ft.)

Inner view of city walls of Sian showing the ramps the defenders used to climb to the ramparts. Total height 9 meters.

Gate along the inner line of defensive walls in Northern China.

PLAN OF PEKING

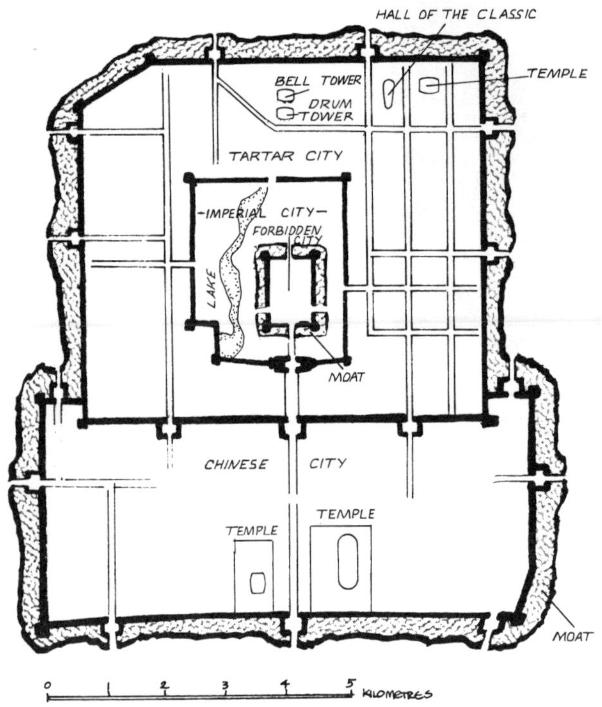

WALLS AROUND TATAR CITY
10 - 12 METERS HIGH

WALLS AROUND CHINESE CITY
5 - 8 METERS HIGH

THE WALLS VARY IN THICKNESS FROM
12 - 21.3 METERS

PEKING GATE FROM CHINESE CITY TO TARTAR CITY

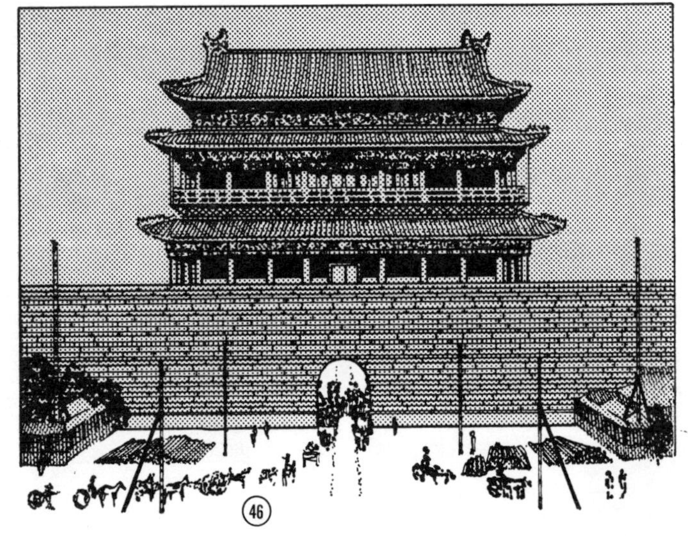

THE CENTRAL GATE IN THE WEST WALL OF THE CITY OF TARTAR.

Peking

Barbican of the central gate in the west wall of the city.

Total height of wall approximately 10 meters.

Barbican 20 meters.

FLOOR PLAN OF THE ABOVE BARBACAN

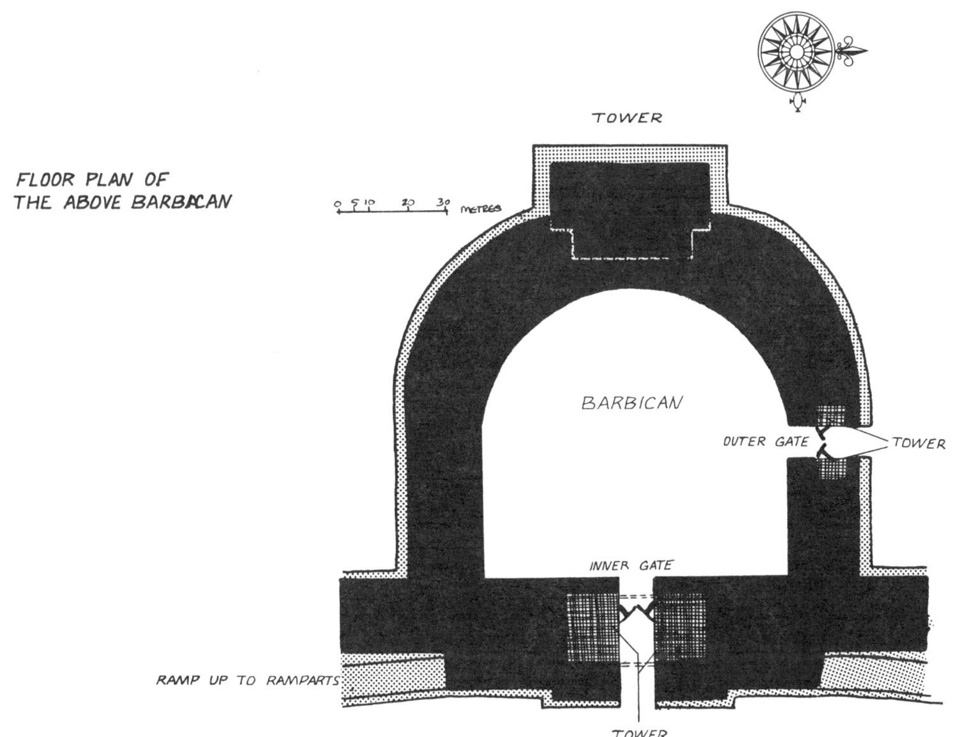

MAP OF
EASTERN ASIA
KOREA
GREAT WALL
JAPAN
China
PHILIPPINE
ISLANDS
MALAY
PENINSULA
equator
BORNEO
NEW
GUNEA
CELEBES
SUMATRA
JAVA
AUSTRALIA

BIBLIOGRAPHY

Anderson, L.J.: Japanese Armour.
Arai, Hakuseki: The Armour Book in Hochō - Gunkikō.
Draeger, Donn R.: Weapons and Fighting Arts of the Indonesian Archipelago.
Needham, Joseph: Science and Civilization in China, Vol. 1&4.
Ratti, Oscar and Westbrook, Adele: Secrets of the Samurai.
Robinson, H. Russel: Oriental Armour.
Stone, George C.: A Glossary of the Construction, Decoration, and Use of Arms and Armour.
Tarassuk, Leonid and Blair, Claude: The Complete Encyclopedia of Arms & Weapons.
Toy, Sidney: A History of Fortification from 3000 B.C. Through 1700 A.D..
Vollmer, John E.: In the Presence of The Dragon Throne.

THE VALLEY OF THE PHARAOHS

The Valley of the Pharoahs is a unique blend of fantasy and history. The setting, civilation and time period are outlined to recreate a realistic flavor. The Egyptians rich beliefs and superstitions in regards to mysticism gods and fantastic creatures all lend themselves to the fantasy aspects.

THE BOXED SET INCLUDES:
50 page rule book with...
- Magick System
- Quick Combat
- Elementary Skills
- 5 Character Classes
- Concise Goods Section
- Brief Monster and Animal Section
- Historical Background
- Hieroglyphs and more!

16 X 20 Color Map of Egypt

3 Black and White Fold Out Maps

Fold-Out Floor plans - layouts of...
- The True Pyramid
- The Giza Necropolis
- The Step Pyramid
- Temple of Hatshepsut
- Temple at Karnak
- Simple Types of Fortifications
- City Fortifications
- Domestic Houses
- Boats of the Nile
- Character Sheet

Box Set: $12.00 (post paid)
Rule Book (only): $6.95 (post paid)

Palladium Books
5669 Casper
Detroit, MI 48210